Miracle Road

A TRUE STORY OF FAITH FOR HEALING
AND RESTORATION

Angela Adkins
with Jessica Errico

TRILOGY CHRISTIAN PUBLISHERS
TUSTIN, CA

Trilogy Christian Publishers

A Wholly Owned Subsidary of Trinity Broadcasting Network

2442 Michelle Drive

Tustin, CA 92780

For information, address Trilogy Christian Publishing

Rights Department, 2442 Michelle Drive, Tustin, Ca 92780.

Trilogy Christian Publishing/ TBN and colophon are trademarks of Trinity Broadcasting Network.

For information about special discounts for bulk purchases, please contact Trilogy Christian Publishing.

Cover image: Photo by Andrew Neel from Pexels

10 9 8 7 6 5 4 3 2 1

Library of Congress Cataloging-in-Publication Data is available.

ISBN 978-1-64088-664-3

ISBN 978-1-64088-665-0 (ebook)

Endorsements

"*Miracle Road* is a must-read for all who desire to encounter the healing power of the Gospel of Jesus Christ. Angela Adkins artfully communicates how Jesus can, and will, break through your impossible situation with His limitless power. Miracle Road will build your faith, strengthen your hope, and prepare you for victory! Get ready to be gripped with Angela's powerful story of God's faithfulness to heal and apply it to your own Miracle Road!"

Steve Hannett
Author, *Unleashing Heaven's Breath*
Host, *The Miraculous Life TV Show*
Pastor, Abundant Grace Church, Rutherford, NJ
President, EveryHouse Ministries
https://www.stevehannett.com/

"*Miracle Road* is not only a true story, but is also a book that will take you deep into the heart and mind of God for your own healing, or for someone you love. I know Angela Adkins personally, and her passion is to see people set free by God's healing power through His son, JESUS CHRIST, and by the power of the Holy Spirit. As you read through the chapters of this powerful book, you will see how God's power is available to anyone who will trust Him, and how you can also experience the healing power of God in your own life. This book is a true blessing, and the perfect gift for anyone who is going through a hard time and needs healing in their spirit, mind and body. I highly recommend this book!"

Lisa Buldo
Ordained Minister, Certified Biblical Health Coach,
Author, Speaker, Mentor"
Host, *The Victorious Life TV Show*
www.LisaBuldo.com

"If you don't believe in God and Miracles, you will after reading this amazing book! Angela's story is a testimony of hope, strength and perseverance, demonstrating that when we believe that something is not possible, GOD MAKES IT POSSIBLE. Find a comfortable chair because you are not going to want to put this book down once you start!"

"The book *Miracle Road*, is an incredible story of a 14-year-old teenage life of faith in the midst of tragedy, hardship, and pain. Angela shares her faith, struggles, frustrations, and joys throughout the remarkable recovery of her terrible ordeal. As you read this book, you will feel the emotions of her roller coaster ride in her journey and see the miracles that God performed in her remarkable road to recovery. It is a powerful book of encouragement for everyone to read."

"While tragic stories are found everyday all around the globe, very few ever include the amount of faith found in Angela's story. If you're at a hopeless point in your life, then you need to hear her story. If you've experienced hurt and have convinced yourself that God can never use you, then you need to hear her story. If you've given up on God all together, then you need to hear her story. It's a story of tremendous hurt and pain, yet a story of victory. It's a story that shows how God's glory can shine through even the darkest moments of your life."

Pastor Scott Clevenger
Lead Pastor/Connection Point Church
Pensacola, FL
Author, *Drift: How to Defeat Accidental Drift In Your Life*
https://connectionpointpensacola.com

Contents

Dedication

To my wonderful family ~
who walked this Miracle Road with me:
my parents, Lowell and Shirley Hicks; my sister, Renea
Zachary;
and my husband,
Robert Adkins.

My parents with my sister and me.

Your love and support
made this book possible!
I love you.

ANGELA ADKINS

Introduction

Only God knows the roads we will travel through life. He sees the events and people, trials and blessings that comprise our earthly journeys. I'm so grateful that He is in control and that He moved my family to southeastern coastal Georgia in the winter of 2011. If He hadn't, I wouldn't have met a very special lady. Angela Adkins is one of those rare people who exudes who she really is and welcomes others to be real as well. When our paths crossed at a local ministry, I sensed immediately a kindred spirit.

Her eyes twinkle and her smile is infectious. In feminine dress, with her hair styled just so, she is not only attractive but winsome. The day we met, her uneven gait (and the arm crutches that assist her to walk) were the very last things I noticed. Though I was curious about her crutches, I had to wait until our third meeting to hear about what she had survived. The miracles she experienced inspire awe in a supernatural God. How incredible that He would bring us together, me from central Florida and Angela from Nashville to write her story and share her miracle road with the world.

Angela loves God! She has walked beside Him since she was only four years old. He has been faithful to her during joyful times as well as extremely painful times, getting much glory from her obedient heart. In Matthew's Gospel account we read, "With God all things are possible" (Matthew 19:26). Angela's testimony attests to this very truth! She points to God's miraculous deliverance and gracious care, and longs for you to know Him like she does.

It has been a privilege, as a friend and writer, to collaborate with her on this book. In its pages you will read about the greatness of our God. You'll also encounter sustaining faith. Faith big enough to conquer any obstacle, precious enough to bring rest to any soul, and true enough to transform any life.

My prayer and hope is, as you read about Angela's *Miracle Road*, you will encounter like never before our awesome God and His Son the Lord Jesus Christ. What He has accomplished in her spirit and body, He can also do in me and you. So, set some time aside, grab your favorite beverage, and join us as we brag on the God of the universe.

In His service,
Jessica C. Errico
Author of *THE MOTHER GAP*

Prologue

Have you experienced God's supernatural touch? Or heard about an angel's visit? I am living proof that God does miracles today. He watches over our lives and assists those who love Him. Often, He intersects the lives of strangers for His purposes, preparing His children in advance. And, in the snap of a finger, when you least expect it, your whole life can change. I know. It happened to me.

My name is Angela, and I'm the oldest of two daughters born to Lowell and Shirley Hicks. I'm a preacher's kid, pure and simple. Both my parents are sold out to serving God, and ministry has always been a priority for . me. Even so, like most folks, I've experienced my share of mistakes and mishaps. The wondrous thing is God has never left me.

All of my childhood centered around activities at church. Dad's call to pastor took us to more than 32 states in the United States, and four provinces in Canada. He led 13 churches, three of which he started from the ground up. So on an autumn night in 1987 after serving God's people in a regular Wednesday night service in Bay Springs, Mississippi, nothing seemed unusual as we headed home. We lived in the town of Petal, roughly an hour away. Little did I know Highway 11 would become a miracle road for me. This is what I remember...

It was a warm and humid fall evening, typical for the South. The air was at a stand-still, while bugs circled the lamp posts in a frenzied dance. I ran to the car, hopping into the back of our brand new 1987 Chevrolet Cavalier. It was dark brown with a gold top and a beige interior. I loved that car because it was the first brand-new car my folks had owned since I was born 14 years earlier. The new car smell was intoxicating and, with my learner's permit, I enjoyed any opportunity to drive it! However, it was a school night and past 9, so I didn't get behind the wheel. Instead settling into the back seat next to my sister Renea, we began planning my upcoming 15th birthday celebration, just days away. I remember our happy conversation as we discussed who I would invite to my party, and an upcoming church convention in Birmingham. Life was so exciting for me right then. As I lay my sleepy head against the car window, I felt a deep contentment.

There was no way I could have known that night, October 14, 1987, my life was about to change forever. On the dark country road, midway between Bay Springs and Petal, there was a car crash. I died in the backseat.

Part One

The Crash

"Everything can change in the blink of an eye. But don't worry; God never blinks."

Regina Brett

The headlights of an oncoming car pierced the tranquil night. We were half-way home, traveling on Highway 11, in Moselle. The advancing car was on our side of the two-lane highway, headed straight for us. When it swerved off the road, only minutes from us, Dad thought it was turning down a side road or driveway. Suddenly, the car swerved back into our lane. Dad veered to avoid a head-on collision, but the driver of the other car swerved yet again. This time he smashed into us, impacting the whole right side of our car, exactly where I was sleeping in the backseat. Both windshields shattered, as the passenger side of our car crushed in like a soda can.

After impact, our car spun wildly and careened off the road. The violent momentum propelled us across a field. Our vehicle abruptly stopped within inches of a tree on one side and a propane gas tank on the other. Only God's angels could have kept the car from hitting either of these obstacles, preventing a fiery explosion.

In those first few moments right after the crash, Mom found herself pinned in by the dashboard and the crumpled passenger door. She couldn't move and began to hyperventilate. Concern for her daughters in the back seat overwhelmed her. She tried to call out to us girls, but words wouldn't come out of her mouth. Dad, who had hit the windshield and was bleeding from his forehead, was trying to tend to Mom and calm her down.

As the world stopped spinning, my sister Renea found me lying across her lap, unresponsive. She tried shaking me and slapped my face. Then her guttural screams split the dark night. Unintelligible at first, her shrieks became pleas, "ANGELA! Wake up! Wake up!"

With my lifeless body draped over her legs, she continued to weep, shouting: "She's not responding to me! She's not moving! Mom, Dad, I can't get Angela to wake up!"

When Dad saw what was happening, he jumped out of the car to get into the backseat. Renea was able to move, and made room for Dad by standing right outside the car. Dad grabbed me, shook me, and cried, "Angela! Answer daddy! Please, please Angela! Answer me!" When no response came, he gently lowered me to the seat and quickly ran from the car, screaming for someone to call an ambulance.

"Oh God, Oh God!" he pleaded, "You gave her to us,. Please don't let her die!"

It was said that the horrific sound of the impact was heard over a one-mile radius of the crash site. People responded by leaving their homes to see what happened, wondering if they could help. One fellow approached Dad and told him an ambulance had already been called. Help was on the way. Then he asked if Dad was okay, as blood continued to run down his face.

At this point Dad doesn't remember feeling any pain, just an agonizing fear that his oldest daughter was gone.

He turned back toward our car and noticed someone leaning into the back section hovering over me! Rushing forward he saw the driver of the car that hit us trying to give me mouth-to-mouth resuscitation. Mom, who was still pinned in the front, was snapping at this stranger, telling him to leave me alone. Then Dad, a stout strong man, grabbed him and yanked him off of me. "Leave my daughter alone!" he demanded.

Fighting anger and worried about his family, Dad confronted the man named Steve who caused the crash. As he did so, the stench of alcohol was overwhelming. Instinctively, Dad's heart turned to ministry, sensing Steve needed to know Jesus. He began preaching right there on the side of the road, telling Steve that he needed God's forgiveness. We later found out Steve had been to four bars prior to the crash and had simply passed out at the wheel. He said he never even saw us.

Returning to the car, Dad repositioned himself on the backseat, and Mom managed to turn her body so she could see me better. There had been no response from me at all. I still lay there lifeless as my parents, the God-fearing, faith-filled couple that they are, began to pray for me. They earnestly begged God to spare my life. Their prayer was simple and gut-wrenching:, "Oh God, please! Please! Don't let her die!"

By now there were several folks milling around our car, waiting for the police and EMTs to arrive. As Dad and Mom persisted in prayer, they felt a strong presence enter the car. It was calming and peaceful. My sister recalls the night had been so still, with no breeze at all, when as if in response to our parents' prayers, she felt a patch of wind go right by her.

"Did you feel that?" asked a woman standing next to her.

No doubt it was the Holy Spirit because the car started to shake. Then to everyone's amazement, and in fulfillment of my parents' hope, a gush of air escaped my lips!

After endless minutes passed, it was as if breath was breathed back into my body. The best I can describe the sensation is to liken it to getting "the wind knocked out" of you, and then experiencing a sharp intake of breath.

Without medical personnel at the scene, I was never diagnosed as clinically dead. But based on what my family observed and experienced, I wasn't merely unconscious. Renea affirms I was not breathing, nor had I moved or given any indication of life. Then in response to faith-filled prayers, with witnesses all around the car, I suddenly heard my mother's voice calling to me as if from a distance. You know, like when she'd call us in from playing at dinner time.

"Angela! Angela!" She was calling me back to them.

With the echoes of her voice in my ears, and that first breath filling my lungs, my body groaned with pain.

In the Beginning

*"Know that you were formed by God's hands, dreamed up
in His heart, and placed in this world for a purpose."*
- Anonymous (from Psalms 139:13-16)

In October 1972, fifteen years before the crash, Lowell Hicks fully expected his firstborn child would be a boy. No particular reason; it just seemed natural to expect a son. In fact, as he recalls, he and Shirley only had a boy's name in mind when he drove her to the hospital in labor. Sometimes I think when God watches us, He has a real chuckle!

From the beginning of their marriage, my parents were eager to start a family. They delighted in spoiling their nieces and nephews, often hanging out with them and hosting sleep overs. Yet, as the years rolled by, Mom couldn't help wondering why she hadn't conceived. She and Dad took their desire for a child to the Lord, praying for His blessing. In the meantime, they also ministered to neighborhood children, bringing them to church services and blessing them with their focused attention. Then came the moment when their prayers were answered! To say they were overjoyed when Mom discovered she was pregnant, right around their third wedding anniversary would be the greatest understatement.

Pregnancy brought its own set of challenges, and Mom, like millions of women before her, battled a periodic concern for her unborn child. One of her friends had just recently lost a baby, and the enemy of our souls cunningly uses such situations to target mothers-to-be with fear. To combat this, Mom was faithful in prayer, asking God to protect her baby and bring her through a healthy pregnancy. She regularly read scripture over me while I was in her womb, wanting to plant the seed of God's Word in my heart before I was even born.

Not long before she delivered me, Mom had a dream of a little girl in a beautiful dress, holding a white Bible. Since another friend had just announced her pregnancy, Mom assumed the dream was about that young woman. However, it turned out to be a prophetic vision about me! Since sonograms were not regularly prescribed in the 1970s, Mom and Dad didn't know God had formed me as a girl. Nor could they know He would indeed use me to share the good news of the Gospel with others.

On October 25th, one of those glorious Tennessee autumn days, Mom went into labor. The air was crisp and the trees were lovely, adorned with festive orange and red leaves. My folks were excited and hopeful, eager to be parents. They weren't aware of the travail ahead of them, but trusted in the goodness of God to walk them through whatever came.

Back in 1972, at Bradley Memorial Hospital in Cleveland, Tennessee, expectant fathers weren't invited to keep their wives company during labor and delivery. So, alongside other fathers-to-be, Dad paced the floor of the small waiting area, nearly wearing out the linoleum tiles. Both my grandmothers and other family members waited with him, everyone a bit nervous that I was taking so long to make my debut.

Mom had a prolonged and difficult labor. Her young doctor feared I was in the breech position. He warned Dad that Mom was in for a long haul as they waited for me to turn in the right direction. Mom shared a room with another lady in labor and their contractions seemed to come in tandem, their deep groans and screams heard down the hallway. This was distressing for Dad, but he remembers that often after a contraction would ease, he'd hear laughter coming from their room. At one point he wondered aloud, "What are they doing? Sounds like they're having a party."

An amazing thing happened during Mom's difficult labor. A sweet nurse repeatedly came into the room in response to Mom's cries of pain. The nurse would gently massage Mom's abdomen, soothing her by her presence. Mom thought it odd that the nurse only ministered to her, never attending the other woman sharing the room. Then, after Mom labored all through the night and most of the day, the doctor informed Dad a C-section was necessary. This same caring nurse accompanied Mom while she was taken down the hallway to the operating room, yet was never seen again. Dad hadn't met this special caregiver because he hadn't been in the room with Mom. Later when he tried to help find this "nurse" to thank her, the hospital said no one matched her description!

When birth doesn't go exactly as one plans, which is often the case, God's love is an anchor against fear and pain. Mom and Dad were secure in His mighty hands and totally dependent on Him for the little son they expected.

Imagine everyone's surprise when after many, many hours, a nurse entered the waiting area, pronouncing: "Congratulations Mr. Hicks! You are the proud father of a baby girl!"

Stunned for a second, Dad wondered, who me? Under his breath he muttered, "I have a baby girl?"

The world stopped as realization set in. With a slightly stronger voice he affirmed, "I have a baby girl." Then joy erupted and he jumped out of his seat, yelling: "I HAVE A BABY GIRL!" Everyone in the waiting room laughed at Dad's reaction, showering him with warm hugs and smiles of congratulations.

In fact, many family members and friends came to celebrate my birth. During the typical eight days that women stayed in the hospital after a cesarean section back then, my folks were overwhelmed by a deluge of loving wishes, prayers and gifts. Tickled with their new family, they nicknamed me their little "Pumpkin" because of my October birthdate. But I still needed an official name.

It was interesting to find out in the course of writing this book that Mom had actually selected a girl's name prior to my arrival. "Just in case," she mused. After looking through a book of baby names, the one that really appealed to her was "Angela." Looking back, she believes that this decision was tied to her dream of the sweet little girl holding the white Bible, and confirmed by her gratitude for the mysterious, angelic helper who had just recently assisted her during labor. The name Angela is Latin, of Christian origin, derived from the Greek word *ángelos* (αγγελος), meaning "messenger of gods." It was a popular girl's name between 1965 and

1979, though I only knew one other girl with the same name as I grew up. My dad selected my middle name "Michelle," after one of my cousins. Michelle comes from the French, meaning "who is like God," and is the female version of the name Michael, like the archangel in scripture.

Thousands of years ago in the Book of Psalms, King David wrote the following about how God created him in his mother's womb: *My frame was not hidden from you when I was made in the secret place, when I was woven together in the depths of the earth. Your eyes saw my unformed body; all the days ordained for me were written in your book before one of them came to be.*

Psalm 139:15-16 (NIV)

Truly God has had His hand on all of us from conception, the very beginning of our lives.

I praise Him for forming me and ordaining my days. True to Mom's vision, my days revolve around sharing God's Word with others. And what a comfort to know, without a shadow of doubt, He was with me during the crash that changed the course of my life.

Aftermath

"We can walk through the darkest night with the radiant conviction that all things work together for the good."
                                        - Martin Luther King

My groans of pain were music to my parents' ears. They didn't know the extent of my devastating injuries, but at that moment, relief flooded their hearts to know I was alive. God was with them. They could feel the assurance of His presence, even as fear continued to taunt their thoughts. Standing there on the side of that dark road, willing the first responders to arrive on the scene, Dad recalled a passage of scripture written by the apostle Paul in the Book of Romans, chapter 8 and verse 28 (NKJV). Paul wrote, *"And we know that all things work together for the good to those who love God, to those who are called according to His purpose"*. Dad stood on those words as God's personal promise to him. He chose to believe that everything would turn around and would be used for God's good in our lives.

Weeks prior to the crash, Dad had sensed God comforting him with these words: *"This too shall pass".* Until the events of that night, he couldn't comprehend what the Holy Spirit was trying to communicate. Then in light of this terrible trial, and all the uncertainty facing us, Dad understood. God promised that He was going to turn this tragedy around for our good.

I believe at the moment my family sensed the sweet presence of God fill the car, HE touched me. His Spirit swept over my lifeless body, breathed on me, and brought me back to life. How loving and merciful was that!

God spared my life, leaving me here for a reason. Could it be to tell of His amazing grace and love for all His children? To share that in this vast universe He created, He cares for each one of us, no matter how big or how small.

All at once, the scene of the crash went from dreadfully still to bustling. After what seemed like an eternity, we were suddenly surrounded by an ambulance, fire truck, and police cars. As valiant first-responders quickly assessed our situation, they confirmed that Mom was indeed pinned in the car unable to get out. Though she would need quick attention, they immediately turned their focus toward me and began to work with me first.

Checking my vitals and injuries, the EMTs determined they needed to life-flight me to Forest General Hospital as quickly as possible. Forest General Hospital was 20 minutes away by ambulance, so they radioed for Rescue 7 to come get me. Next they lifted me on to a gurney, placed my neck in a brace and strapped me down from head to toe. Once the helicopter arrived, and I was deemed ready for take-off, the EMTs began to assess the rest of my family.

The sights and sounds of my first helicopter flight were lost to me. The dark night sky and whirl of the helicopter blades would have fascinated me if I wasn't in shock and drifting in and out of consciousness. I barely remember someone asking me my name. I answered, "Angela." Then the man asked me routine questions such as: "How old are you?"

I said, "14." He asked, "Where were you coming from?" I said, "Bay Springs." And finally, "Where were you going?" To which I answered, "To my home in Petal." Then the blackness returned.

The whole ordeal seemed like a dream to me, a horrible nightmare without any basis in reality. I didn't know who was asking me questions or why he was asking them. I just complied and answered. I don't remember feeling any pain, but according to my family, I was groaning the whole time they were working on me, even screaming out several times. Yet, I wasn't aware of any of this, or even my arrival at the hospital. All I actually remember, apart from the man's questioning, is seeing bright lights and hearing my mother's voice.

Isn't God good to give us a reprieve from trauma? He designed our bodies with mechanisms to spare us some of the most hurtful and grievous memories. I so appreciate His tender care for me, and all the prayers that ascended to His throne the night of the crash and throughout these ensuing 30 years.

Back at the crash scene my family was extremely concerned about me, each of them asking the paramedics if I would be all right. Mom said that as they pulled me out of the car, she could tell something was wrong with my hip. She said my left leg seemed a lot shorter than my right leg. In her mother's heart, she knew something was badly broken. Still, the EMTs reassured her that I would be all right.

My sister Renea received the same encouragement from those attending to her. However, she recalls the alarm she felt when they put me on the gurney. From her vantage point, she noticed that my hip looked very unusual. She told me that it was as if the bone was sticking through the back side of my clothes. Though my bone never broke through the skin, she said it looked like it had totally dislocated. Again, she drilled the paramedics about my welfare. Those patient first responders sure had their hands full with us that night!

When the policeman arrived on the scene, he approached Dad first to find out what happened and then addressed the drunk driver standing nearby. Since the extent of Steve's intoxication was obvious, the officer immediately arrested and handcuffed him, confronting him with his heinous actions. He proceeded to shake Steve a bit, who was old enough to have a son my age, and then put him in the back of the police car with the stern warning "not to move a muscle!"

It only took a short while for the policeman to record all the details of the crash. Renea remembers dad telling her and mom that the officer was furious about the fact that Steve was drinking and driving, while not even possessing a valid license due to previous offenses. He told dad he could just chew him up and spit him out.

We've learned police officers are passionate about DUI crimes as are paramedics and firefighters who arrive first on scene. These first responders see so much devastation and senseless tragedy caused by alcohol-related crashes. Drunken driving is a 100 percent preventable crime. It has grave emotional impact on victims and rescue workers as well.

When the EMT assessed Dad's condition, he was quick to say he was fine. He didn't want to be strapped to a gurney and the medical personnel relented. However, Dad was still bleeding from his face due to the broken glass of the windshield. He asked if he could ride up front in the ambulance, which was a perfect plan because Mom and Renea were in the back. That way they could all ride together, and an additional ambulance wasn't needed.

Finally, focus was turned to my sister's condition, while firefighters worked on getting the passenger door open so Mom could be freed. Before the paramedics arrived, after I started breathing again, one of the townsfolk had brought a chair for Renea. Her legs were scratched up from shattered back window glass and one of them felt very stiff. She was having trouble bending it, so the thoughtful provision of a chair was a special blessing!

I'm told they put her on a flat board called a back board. They also put her neck in a brace and strapped her down. She recalls how uncomfortable the board was, and that when they lifted her into the ambulance, they locked the board to the interior of the vehicle. At this point the firefighters were still working on Mom's door and almost had it open. Renea could watch the scene unfold from where she was laying. After a paramedic reassured her that she was okay, he joined the others attending Mom.

A humorous situation arose regarding some tape the paramedic placed on Renea's forehead. It wasn't comfortable at all, and my sister started to stress about its location across her eyebrows. What if when they peeled off the tape at the hospital, her eyebrows came off too?

In comical fashion, she began fingering the adhesive, freeing it from her brow line. No way was she going to lose her eyebrows if at all possible! I still smile when I think of this scenario today and am so grateful that when she shared it with me many years ago, we laughed out loud.

It is Renea, so close to my age and truly frightened, who remembers most of the details of that fateful night. Mom and Dad were so focused on prayer for God to heal me, that their minds registered little else. For instance, Mom can barely recall the car door coming off or being strapped onto a gurney and lifted into the ambulance. Dad remembers talking with EMTs about me, desperately wanting reassurance that I would be all right. They graciously affirmed the doctors at the hospital would take very good care of me.

Renea remembers being told in the ambulance that paramedics don't usually turn on their sirens or lights unless their patients are in life-threatening situations, and thankfully the three of them were not. Yet in this case, with the urgent need to reunite them with me at the hospital as soon as possible, they would make an exception and use the sirens and lights. In an effort to further cheer and distract Renea, one paramedic said he wished he had let her ride in the chopper with me. However, as we later learned, that would have been impossible because there wouldn't have been enough room. Still, the team's calm conversation and gentle questions made the trip bearable. We all received excellent care.

Author Rex Rouis writes, "Faith comes alive when the word read from the page becomes the word heard in your heart." As my family was transported to safety, not knowing what to expect about my condition, they clung to faith in our gracious and loving Heavenly Father and recited His promises from memory in their hearts. Even so, Mom felt it took forever to get to her firstborn's side.

Growing Up Angela

"For Beautiful Eyes look for the good in others. For Beautiful Lips speak only words of kindness. And for Poise, walk with the knowledge that you are never alone."

- Audrey Hepburn

My life as the firstborn daughter was never once dull nor boring. My parents adored me, and just eleven months after I arrived, they gave me the best present ever: a baby sister! Prior to her birth, Dad answered the call to pastor a church in Bradenton, Florida, so we moved from Cleveland, Tennessee, when I was five months old. Renea was born in Bradenton six months later. I loved helping Mom with the new baby and became Mom's "runner," fetching things she needed and making her smile. Truly, I can't remember life without Renea by my side.

My childhood was full of family, faith and friends. I'll never take for granted the joy I experienced as I grew up. The rural South in the 1970s was a much safer place to grow up in than most children experience today. Our imaginations soared as we planned outside adventures, swinging on swings and climbing trees. I remember when we were in elementary school, Mom would allow us to join with friends and walk half a mile down the road to buy penny candy. Little did we know what a treat it was! That touch of independence is something many children don't get to enjoy today. It makes me sad to think that many don't have the same opportunities we had because contemporary culture is so different, and because children spend so much time plugged in to online devices.

Mom says that because I was obedient and responsible, she wasn't concerned as Renea followed me about. In fact, I kept her occupied riding bikes, running and making up games. I learned to play badminton and tennis with the many friends and cousins that frequently visited.

We really enjoyed it when Mom joined in with us. It was a good thing that Renea and I liked people because there wasn't a shortage of folks in and out of our home.

Even though I was an active, athletic kid, I was also a "girly-girl." Dresses were my preferred style of clothing, then and today as well. Even as a little girl I loved to play "dress-up" with jewelry, high heels, and purses. My affinity for accessories and feminine styling continues. I guess once a girly- girl, always a girly-girl.

Another distinction of my childhood was how we celebrated birthdays. In our family, birthday parties were themed events. Mom was tireless in hosting joyful gatherings to please us and make wonderful memories. There was always a big group of children excited to be invited over to our house. One year, since my birthday is in October, we had a costume party, and I remember dressing up as an 80's Pop Star! I put on a washed-out jean skirt and a white shirt with a bright yellow fish-net top over it. Fluffing out my hair, I sprayed it with a temporary pink color, and lined my arms with Jelly bracelets. How fun to rock the starlet image, if only for a day. Such fun times stoked a yearning in me to be a model or an actress.

I was very young when God gave me a desire to make music, and the ability to play by ear. I would spend hours plunking out tunes on the piano. My interest was recognized by church pianists and a couple of them taught me basic chords and techniques. So, without any formal training, I was playing in church by age nine! By the time I was 12 years old, I was filling in for the regular piano player. At subsequent churches, I took on that whole responsibility. Not only is music ministry something I've continued for nearly four decades, but God also enabled me to teach Renea how to play. Later, when I married and moved away, she could take over as pianist and song leader.

Almost as much as playing the piano, I've loved to sing. What a joy to perform gospel hymns for church congregations and nursing home residents. My folks tell the story of how they placed me upfront at the altar to sing before the church when I was only two years old. From that moment, young as I was, I knew what it felt like to brighten peoples' day and enjoy their affirmation. Of course, just as soon as she was able, Renea had to be in the picture too. Imagine for a minute, the two of us standing up front in our pretty little dresses, singing for the congregation. As folks craned to see us (we've always been on the shorter end of the height chart) I would carry the melody while Renea joined in on the last word of every line, belting it out! Needless to say, we both blossomed as Mom and Dad encouraged us to use our budding talents to serve God and His people.

Indeed, ours was a family ministry. Often when Dad would evangelize he depended on Mom, me and Renea to supply music and song. There were times when we needed to fill in with drama too, such as at Christmas. It was a good thing that I enjoyed acting because I was involved in countless Christmas plays, later coordinating several myself. Summers brought Vacation Bible School sessions, which were always a highlight for me and the other youngsters of our church. Obviously, my relationship with Jesus began when I was so, so young. Some might question if a preschooler can give his or her life to Christ, so let me describe what happened to me.

We had moved to Delaware in May 1977, so Dad could pastor a little white church, the Full Gospel Church on Jewel Street in Delmar. Originally a country Methodist church, it had large beautiful stained-glass windows, and hardwood floors adorned with carpet runners. On the platform was a beige carpet with a floral pattern, and the benches for the congregation were delicately styled in wood. A week-long revival event was wrapping up, led by Brother Charles McNevin, the General Overseer for the Church of God House of Prayer, which was our denomination.

It had been one of those glorious spring weeks, when the air is resplendent, the temperature just perfect, and a sense of hope almost tangible. Brother McNevin was in his '70s, a stately man of God, with striking white hair and always impeccably dressed. As they say in church circles, he "walked the walk and talked the talk," meaning he lived the life of a true Christ follower. Well respected by the churches under his supervision, his love and care for God's people was genuine. As he preached during that week in May 1977, the powerful presence of God filled our little packed-out church, saving souls and changing lives.

On the final night of revival services, with the chill of winter long gone and the hot, humid summer soon approaching, it seemed even nature was rejoicing in the goodness of God. No one, however, had an inkling of how my life would change and most definitely not me. I was only four years old, and though my parents were raising me in church, teaching me about God's love and His mighty works, I had not yet surrendered my heart to God or invited Christ into my life.

After this particular service, as was his custom, Brother McNevin gave the altar call. He asked if anyone in the congregation wanted to come forward and receive salvation through faith in Jesus. Now, because of my father's ministry and our close relationship with Brother NcNevin and his wife, I wasn't intimidated to approach him, but I was not planning to leave my seat. Yet, this wasn't a normal church service for me. I became aware of God's Spirit tugging at my heart. How amazing that the God of the universe cares so much about us that He woos our hearts, no matter what age.

Suddenly I found myself walking down the aisle to the altar, with my parents quickly following after me. Picture this feminine little four-year-old with long brown hair and expectant brown eyes standing before Brother McNevin, who towered over me. With Dad and Mom on either side of me, I declared, "I want to get saved."

Smiling, Brother NcNevin put his large hand on my forehead and began to pray for me. Mom peeked my way and saw my little arms go up, raising my hands in the air to worship God as tears streamed down my face. Both my parents and the pastor began to cry as well. After we prayed, Brother McNevin asked me this question in front of the congregation, "Angela, what just happened to you?"

I replied with tear bright eyes, "I got saved!" Everyone in the church cheered!

Later that night, when the house was settled and quiet, Mom remembers the nagging thought that I might be too young to understand what it meant to give my life to Christ. She prayed as she fell asleep that God would show her I truly understood the meaning of what I had done. His answer came early the next day. In the morning, I padded down the hardwood steps of our home to join my parents for breakfast. They both noticed I was wiping tears from my eyes and asked me why I was crying.

"I had a dream about Jesus," I answered. "He was hanging on the cross, but then He looked straight at me and said, 'Angela, I love you and I died for you!'"

Of course, my parents' hearts leapt for joy. Their firstborn had made a true commitment to Christ, and Mom knew my dream was confirmation of her secret prayer. Not only had I given my heart to Jesus, but he also revealed himself to me and spoke directly to me. Christ was living in me because I accepted the sacrifice He made for me, and I trusted Him to come into my heart. They shared my dream with Brother McNevin who was over-joyed as well. He remembered sensing that God had His Hand on me in a special way ever since I was a baby. As it is written in Psalms 139, God knew the plans He had for me before I was born; plans that began to unfold early in my life.

Even now, when I think about Jesus on the cross and the blood He shed for each one of us, I am humbled by His obedience to suffer and die for me. In the dream I had as a little girl, I remember seeing clearly the nails in His hands and feet, and blood flowing from them. I saw the crown of thorns on His head as blood ran down his face. That God, our Heavenly Father, would decree the perfect blood of Jesus is sufficient to bring redemption for our sins and healing to our lives is almost too wonderful to grasp.

Thousands of years before Christ was crucified, the Prophet Isaiah wrote the following: *But he was pierced for our transgressions, he was crushed for our iniquities; the punishment that brought us peace was on him, and by his wounds we are healed.*

Isaiah 53:5 (NIV)

The only perfect, righteous man to ever walk this earth gave His life to pay the penalty of our sin. Jesus, the Lamb of God, died so we could have abundant life. Check out His words in the Book of John, chapter 10:10 (NKJV). Jesus tells us, *"The thief does not come except to steal, and to kill and to destroy. I have come that they may have life and that they may have it more abundantly."*

By His blood our sins are washed away. By His blood we have peace, and by His blood we are healed!

*My Mom holding my sister and me. I'm pointing at the
camera and smiling from ear to ear.*

My Dad holding me.

My parents with me.

My family and I with my Grandma Hicks.

My 5th Grade School Picture.

Part Two

Part Two

A New Reality

"A strong person is not one that doesn't cry. A strong person is one who cries and sheds tears for a moment, then gets back up and fights again."

Anonymous

By the time the ambulance arrived with my family, doctors were already giving me a second unit of blood. I was in bad shape, having received the brunt of the crash impact. When the offender's vehicle struck us, the sheer force slung my body backward and forward so quickly that it virtually snapped me in two. Just imagine a bull whip as it is cracked! That's the best description I know to explain what the impact did to my petite frame. My back was broken, damaging my spinal cord. My right collar bone was broken, left hip dislocated, and my pelvis was fractured in six places. Much of my body was broken up. In fact, I still remember the deep pain I felt even a week later, while trying to take a deep breath.

But God!

Faith in Him brings hope to any situation. Nothing is impossible for Him. To "see" through eyes of faith is to rest in a different dimension. In stark contrast to the white walls and antiseptic reality of the hospital room, in rebellion against man's finite reasoning, faith is a vibrant frequency all its own.

Prayer is the connection point between God and His people. Dad and Mom had already reached out to friends to pray for me. What started with desperate urgency, quickly became a groundswell of heartfelt petitions for God to heal me. The frequency of faith was vibrating among all who knew my family. They poured out their concern and love for us during this time before cell phones or texting was available. As more folks heard about my situation, they followed up by calling the hospital. I can't even imagine how jammed the switchboard became! Friends and family were calling for updates, and Dad was running back and forth in the emergency waiting room to answer the phones. Renea remembers that if our parents couldn't get to a ringing phone quick enough, they would invariably hear a staff member holler from down the hall, "Is there a Lowell Hicks in the waiting room?"

The power of God unleashed through prayer was a great comfort to my family. I praise Him first for taking care of all three of them that night. After several tests, their triage showed only minor injuries and they were released to go home. Of course, they opted to stay with me. They had to wait in the emergency room, however, until early morning to get the first prognosis of my condition.

This is what the doctor said, "I have good news and bad news. The good news is that at this point your daughter is not facing a life-threatening situation. But, if for some reason surgery had to be done right away, it could be life-threatening because Angela has lost so much blood. The bad news is, she is paralyzed from the waist down. And she may never walk again."

She may never walk again! What horrible words for any parent to hear. Yet, for hours my parents had been praying diligently for me and pressing into faith that God would not only protect me, but heal me. This news, which could have undone them, served to bolster their stance on the eternal promises of God. They sought Him as the source of the recovery their precious, active daughter needed. Knowing I had big plans for my future, they steadied themselves in the face of this very grim diagnosis.

Dad asked the doctor if he would give him a 50 percent chance that I would walk again? The doctor quickly replied, "No. I can't do that. All I can give you is a 1 in 10 chance." To underscore my situation the doctor added, "Mr. Hicks, Angela is hurt really bad. I've seen many patients with these same injuries, and they have never walked again."

Faith kicked into overdrive as Dad looked the doctor straight in the eyes and said, "Well, you don't know the God I serve!"

The doctor, in turn, eyed Dad like he was crazy. He most likely pitied my father, who no doubt was still in shock. Yet, Dad didn't back down and he didn't lose heart. Instead, my folks increased the call to prayer! Phone calls were made to extended family, friends and past congregants asking them to petition God for my healing. Only one friend was able to come up to the hospital that night; however, a multitude joined their hearts with my parents to support us. Our church family and Christians from all over the country stood with us in trusting that God's purposes and plans for my life would override the doctor's prognosis. Truly, God showered us with His love through the concerned prayers of many. We were comforted far more than we ever thought possible in light of the situation.

At this point, I was becoming more aware of the terrible pain caused by my injuries. I guess the shock of the impact was wearing off, and I was able to verbalize through my screams what was hurting the most. Even today I am grateful for God's grace to me, as I doubt I could have endured the nightmare I was facing or the incredible pain without His presence.

While my parents continued to mobilize praying friends, another doctor came to talk to them. He told my dad that he needed papers signed because he needed to do an emergency/exploratory surgery right away. My dad quickly answered, "But, the other doctor said that surgery may be life-threatening!"

"Yes, it may be," replied the doctor. "But she is expressing pain in her stomach, which indicates either her spleen or her intestines are damaged. If we don't find and correct the problem, it also will be life-threatening." Dad signed the papers, continuing to pray while still calling people to join him.

It is so difficult to put myself in my parents' shoes, to appreciate all they were experiencing during those first 24 hours. The crash had completely blindsided them. In the face of the unthinkable, their firstborn was dead in the back of their crumpled car, and all they could do was call out to the Lord with anguished pleas. His Holy Spirit answered their prayers of faith, and I was miraculously resuscitated before their eyes. Now they needed more miracles of healing that only God could do!

The Bible says: *"Trust in the LORD with all your heart, and lean not on your understanding; in all your ways submit to Him and He will make your paths straight."*

Proverbs 3:5-6 (NIV)

God's words in the scriptures proved a strong anchor for all that lay ahead.

By now it was 2 a.m. the morning following the crash. In the operating room, the scrub nurses were preparing me for surgery. Just as the anesthesiologist was getting ready to put me to sleep, the doctor said something told him to touch my stomach one more time. Prior to this, the slightest touch caused me to cry out in pain. This time, however, I did not scream. In fact, there was no sign of pain on my face at all! Puzzled, and concerned the nurses might think him crazy for calling them in, he pressed on my abdomen more firmly. Still no pain.

"Angela, does this hurt?" he asked.

"Not like it did before," I responded.

Immediately he cancelled the surgery plans and walked out of the operating room. When Mom first saw him exit to the hallway, she thought: *Oh no! What could have happened?* But then she noticed a big smile on his face. He told my parents that he couldn't explain what happened; only that their daughter was no longer in excruciating abdominal pain.

"Well, I know what happened." said Mom, "There are people all around the country praying for her right now!" To which he sincerely responded: "Well, keep it up. It's working." That physician checked on me for three days. I never had any more trouble with my stomach, and he agreed there was nothing wrong with my torso or internal organs. I had been healed. Looking back, I know beyond a shadow of doubt, that when the doctor said something told him to assess me one more time, it was God! He healed my stomach instantly.

My family remembers all this activity in the emergency department, but I don't. My first concrete memories start with waking up in ICU. Anything that happened after I leaned against the car door and fell asleep, the crash and its aftermath, was lost to me. However, I quickly became aware of all the tubes running into my body. Also, my left leg was in traction. Groggy, I focused on Mom's face.

"Mom, where am I? What happened?" I asked.

She briefly told me that we had been in a crash. With a tentative smile, she told me everyone was all right and I would be just fine. The doctor had cautioned my family that it would be best not to tell me I was paralyzed for at least the first few days. So, when I promptly asked her, "Why can't I move my legs?," she wanted to stem any feeling of despair.

She began adjusting the covers around my legs and feet, asking me if that made it better. At first, I replied with a tentative "Yes." But as I struggled to move my lower body, panic took over and I screamed, "Oh God! Why can't I move my legs?"

At that point, my family began to cry as grief washed over all of us. Dad, standing by my bed, reached down to look me in the eyes, steadying me with his love. As tears flowed, he told me, "Angela, you are hurt pretty bad. But do you remember the scripture in the Bible that says where any two agree touching any one thing it shall be done?"

I told him I did remember that. He asked me if I believed it was true. I told him I did believe it. "Well," he said, "let's agree and believe together." So, he took my hand and we started praying. Along with my dad, I grabbed a hold of faith which is the gift of God, believing I would come through this and I determined to never let go!

Mom, in the meantime, was praying for a sign I would be fine and that I would walk again. Shortly afterwards, one of the nurses came to her and said, "Now, don't get alarmed, but Angela feels a tingling sensation in her legs."

Then Mom grabbed a hold of faith too! She knew deep in her heart God was going to bring me through this trauma. In fact, I remember after they finally moved me to a room, and I started becoming more aware of where I was and what was going on, I noticed ink marks on my limbs. When I asked the nursing staff why they were there, I was told they were marking me every time I indicated more feeling in my legs. By that point I had feeling down to my knees! I just knew I would have the rest back soon. I really believed it.

Recovery Begins

"The first step towards getting somewhere is to decide that you are not going to stay where you are."

Chauncey Depew

During the days I was in ICU, while God strengthened my body, His people continued to uphold us with prayer and emotional support. The crash occurred years before cell phones, so friends and family had to call the hospital to get updates on my condition. At one point, due to the sheer volume of calls, a nurse at the ICU nurses' station asked Dad, "Can you just sit here at the desk? Every call that comes in is for you anyway." He complied, and sure enough, nearly every call all day long was for us. We were amazed by the multitude of friends and family who prayed for me and my healing. And we were so grateful for the love they poured out on us.

All in all, my stay in ICU is a muddled memory. Most of the time I was sedated and unable to interact with those who came to visit. The heavy-duty medication caused me to feel groggy and my vision was blurry. I was wired up with different tubing, the one that ran down from my nose into my stomach, the most unpleasant. Actually, it was torture! Thirsty all the time, I was frustrated with the ice chips I was allowed to suck on, but then required to spit out. I remember thinking I wouldn't wish this ordeal on anyone.

By the third day I remember saying to Mom, "Please pray they take the tube out of my nose. And pray they move me to a room soon!" Though the nurse had allowed Mom to stay with me around the clock, I was only allowed two visitors at a time. I longed for a room where we could all be together, especially as I became increasingly aware of my surroundings. Mom prayed with me, and it seemed only a few minutes passed before we received great news from the nursing staff. They were getting ready to take the tube out of my nose and move me to a private room! Of course, the tube removal was horrible, but I was so glad to have it over. Soon I was settled in a room where family and friends could hang out with me.

By then we had received the diagnosis that my back was broken in the T12-L1 level (mid to lower back). This explained the damage to my spinal cord. The doctor told us it looked like someone had taken an axe and chopped me in two, then grabbed the separate halves and pulled, shifting them apart. He said one of my vertebrae was crushed as well. He then scheduled the necessary surgery for Monday, my 15th birthday. Needless to say, that became a birthday I will never forget.

It still astounds me to remember how our gracious God sent me wave after wave of encouragement. Stuffed animals, cards, and balloons crowded my room. One nurse even wondered if my bed might begin to float because so many helium balloons were tied to it!

My ordeal became a real community concern. The local newspaper kept up with my progress and town merchants sent gifts with get-well cards. I remember receiving a couple of cosmetic and perfume sets with good wishes for my recovery.

Most importantly, visitors kept coming and praying for me. It seemed every day God's people made us a priority, investing their time to come and support us. We were never alone. I figure I met 14 new preachers who heard about the crash and came to pray for me. No doubt they shared with their prayer groups, increasing the number of times my name was lifted up before God.

Twelve days after the crash, on the morning of my surgery, Dad took off from work and my sister was allowed to miss school. (Mom was always by my side, day and night). Instead of a joyful birthday party with family and friends, I underwent major back surgery with God as the attending physician. Of course, major surgery is traumatic for anyone, and I empathize with all who go under the knife to correct a physical problem. Truly, my teenage heart was devastated. I was trying so hard not to give into fear. With the help of family and friends who came to cheer me on, I made the best of it. With folks crowded around my bed, I was surrounded by singing and prayers and many bright faces expecting the best outcome ever. God promises us a peace that passes understanding, so I focused on Him and not on my anxious thoughts. His comfort was tangible as I sensed His presence with me.

That day was still to be a day of celebration. I later discovered that while I was in surgery one of our friends called into a radio station on my behalf, and I won a birthday cake from the station. Actually, over the course of my birthday weekend, I was given 4 birthday cakes: one from my family, one from friends, one made by the hospital and the one from the radio station!

When they wheeled this birthday girl into the operating room, I hoped for the best birthday gift I could think of, the ability to walk again!

The surgery lasted four and a half hours as I slept through it. Meanwhile, many, many people prayed for me. Doctors inserted stainless steel Harrington rods into my back and removed my crushed vertebrae. They scraped bone from my right hip to stabilize my spine with a bone graft. I came through the extensive procedures with flying colors and rested for two hours in the recovery room.

Then with a hopeful prognosis, I faced the daunting task of rehabilitation. About a week after surgery, having been flat on my back for almost a month, physical therapy began. There were times at first when sitting up made me so dizzy I would be nauseous. I also battled headaches. Occasionally if I sat up for longer than an hour, I'd experience extremely sharp pains that felt as though someone was jabbing me in the back with a knife. Believe it or not, none of this deterred my resolve to get walking again. The pain might halt me temporarily, but it wasn't going to stop me. The therapists and nurses would just put me back to bed, give me some pain medication, and soon I was ready to start the therapy again.

I even developed a plan to cope with all the discomfort. Maybe it was the Holy Spirit's leading, but I had the idea to ask Mom for some bubble gum. When it came time for therapy each day, I'd stick some gum in my mouth. When the pain spiked I wouldn't complain, instead, I'd blow a big bubble! That became my way of releasing the stress and pain of the moment. One of the therapists commented, "We know when Angela is hurting. She doesn't make a peep. We just look up and see a big bubble." This teenage strategy enabled me to press forward with determination. Nothing was going to stop me. My goal was clear and my mind was set: I was going to get well and leave the hospital.

Most of the time I was in good spirits, and looking back, I see how God had prepared me for this challenge from a very young age. As Creator, He gives us specific personality traits to equip us on our life journeys. I believe He blessed me with a sense of deep determination that would keep me in the race.

Even as a little girl, I loved running and racing my friends. Though physical education was my least favorite class in school, I was fast on my feet and competitive. Like most people, I dreaded the team selection process when we would play kickball, baseball or flag football during gym time. Once a game started, I gave my all. Always determined to help my team score and win, my competitive attitude would shine.

One particular school day when I was in fifth grade stands out in my memory. During gym class the teacher said we were going to play flag football and gave us all flags to attach to our clothes at waist height. Our two co-ed teams were instructed there would be no touching, no tripping, and no tackling. The only way to stop a drive to the end zone was to pull an opponent's flag off of them. That constituted a "tackle." At one point the ball was thrown in my direction, I caught it and took off running. With all the practice of my neighborhood running contests, I was moving fast. However, a boy in my class took off after me, grabbed for my flag, missed, and fell to the ground. As he was going down, he wrapped his arms around my legs. Even though it happened quickly, I managed to jump right out of his grip so he didn't trip me. I stayed on my feet and kept running, scoring a touchdown for our team!

That day everyone commented on how I jumped right out of the boy's grip. The teacher immediately scolded him for trying to tackle me, but it really didn't matter because he didn't succeed. What makes the story even funnier is that I was wearing a dress.

Whether it was winning at the Limbo game in school, or pushing myself to bicycle over ten miles one Saturday when I was fourteen, my motto was "Don't give up." Faced with the long recovery ahead, I continually needed to tap into my drive to win, setting my focus on doing my best.

During those first days in the hospital many scriptures were shared with me. Each verse from God's Word was reassuring, and I clung to their truth. The writer of the Book of Proverbs proclaimed:

"Trust in the Lord with all your heart and lean not on your own understanding; In all your ways acknowledge Him and He shall direct your path"

Proverbs 3:5-6 (NKJV).

This passage comforted me because I saw that I couldn't and shouldn't try to figure out why this trial had happened. It directed me not to worry or fret over why the crash occurred, because it was (and is) beyond my understanding. I couldn't lean on what I understood with my natural mind and thoughts, but had to lean on God. These holy words promised me that God would direct me and provide for me as I trusted Him and gave Him glory. While other passages of scripture speak about Him bringing good out of our trials, at that point, I couldn't look into the future and see a hint of what He would accomplish. God was calling me to simply trust Him and do my part in therapy. He knew where He was going to take me next, and He would prove His trustworthiness over and over.

Why Me Lord?

"God's plans for your life far exceed the circumstances of your day."

\- Louie Giglio

Repeatedly through the years I've been asked, "Are you angry at God?"

In fact, just the other day I briefly shared my testimony while concluding a bank transaction. Observing my crutches, the teller asked me if I was mad at God. People want to know if, in light of the crash that so drastically altered my life, I hold God responsible. Friends, health-care workers and new acquaintances who watched my determined battle to regain my mobility sometimes wondered out loud, "Aren't you mad that this has happened to you?"

Even though I believe God is big enough to handle my emotions, and those of all His children, I have never let anger at this situation take hold. Though in our lives there will be times we mourn losses and regret choices, God is not to blame! He is my rock and strength, the One who heals and protects me.

This is not to say frustration and despair didn't try to roost in my heart. I remember one particular day, early in my recovery, when the hardship and challenges before me seemed overwhelming. The insidious question, *Why me?* bombarded my thoughts.

It was a warm November day and I was laying in bed in Forest General Hospital. Mom and Renea were with me and Dad joined us after work so we could all be together. During those first days after my initial back surgery my body hurt all over. The excruciating pain intensified whenever someone touched me. That particular afternoon the hours seemed to drag as we talked, tried to laugh, and attempted to maintain our normal family rhythm. Exhausted from the long weeks of pain and recovery, I was attacked by emotions trying to drag down my spirit.

Suddenly, the walls of my small room seemed to close in on me, squeezing me. The wood paneling behind my bed, the white counter and sink beside me, and the wall with the TV, felt like a gigantic vise. Tears spilled down my face as I realized the pain I was dealing with would take time to resolve; maybe a long time to go away. It wasn't a quick and over kind of hurt, and it required everything I had to conquer it. In those few moments my life felt like a nightmare I wouldn't wish on anyone! Unwelcomed questions crossed my mind and I asked aloud, "Why did this have to happen? Why me? Why did the drunk driver hit us causing all this suffering?"

Dad leaned in close and allowed me to cry. I grabbed a hold of his hand, pouring out the heaviness in my fifteen-year-old heart. "I just don't want to do this anymore," I admitted. Trying to grapple with the unfairness of the whole situation, I told him I was scared and tired of coping with the pain.

Gently Dad affirmed my hurting soul, and then patiently redirected my focus away from the fear and anger that assaulted me. He told me how important it was that I intentionally direct my thoughts to Jesus my loving Savior. He reminded me of all Jesus went through for me; and how He didn't deserve to be nailed to a cross, suffer, or die for us. He did so in obedience to God's plan so our sin would be paid for. "On top of that," he added, "Jesus asked Father God to forgive the very people who crucified Him!"

Standing by my bed, Dad continued to speak truth to me and I could feel my faith strengthening. He emphasized how important it was for me to follow Christ's example. He added, "It's okay to be angry, but don't become bitter. It's okay to admit that you don't understand what happened to you but forgive the person who wronged you. Then Dad went on to share scriptures that point to healing. He referenced Isaiah 53:5 (NKJV) which says: "But he was wounded for our transgressions, he was bruised for our iniquities: the chastisement for our peace was upon him; and by his stripes we are healed." Dad pointed to what the apostle Peter wrote about Jesus: *"Who Himself bore our sins in His own body on the tree, that we, having died to sins, might live for righteousness— BY WHOSE STRIPES YOU WERE HEALED."*

1Peter 2:24 (NKJV)

Jesus' sacrifice brought spiritual, emotional, and physical healing to us. What astounding truth! What miraculous promises! By meditating on these scriptures which are God's Word to us, our thinking is refocused and our minds revitalized. Dad had often quoted the apostle Paul's teaching in the Book of Romans, chapter 12, about renewing our minds with the truths of scripture. Now I needed to be diligent to do just that.

My father went on to tell me, "We are not accepting the doctor's report. We are believing for your total and complete healing. Because by His stripes we are healed!" From that very moment forward, my outlook on my situation was better and life as a whole was easier. I chose to turn my thoughts towards Jesus. I stayed focused on what God was going to do in my life instead of letting circumstances affect me negatively. I determined there was no room for self-defeating thinking in my life and that nothing was going to hold me back from walking again. Truly, my healing process began to accelerate from that point on.

As humans we have an innate sense of justice and are prone to wonder occasionally *Why me?* Difficult circumstances and unfairness trigger that response in us, almost as if sin has hard-wired our DNA to question pain and testing. As I faced my recovery journey head on, that needling question came to the surface a few times. I learned to push it away quickly and focus on the promises of God. Since we all hit bumps along life's path, what a great blessing to know God's Word is true and we can stand firm on His promises!

Faith activates as we stand firm. When we refuse to be swayed by any wind of disappointment or wave of doubt, standing steadfastly on God's Word, the miraculous occurs in our lives! One particular promise is near and dear to my heart. The prophet Jeremiah wrote God's pledge to us in the Old Testament. Speaking for God, he wrote, "'For I know the thoughts that I think toward you,' says the Lord, 'thoughts of peace and not of evil, to give you a future and a hope.'" (Jeremiah 29:11) God's thoughts and plans are to prosper us and not to harm us; to bring about good in our lives. Just as Louie

Giglio teaches, "God's plans for your lives far exceed the circumstances of your day."

Circumstances are only temporary. They will pass! In fact, circumstances are often stepping stones to propel us towards God's purpose and destiny for our lives. However, some situations may not be purposely placed by Him, like the tests He oftentimes uses to help us grow. Such circumstances result from another's mistakes or foolish actions. But no matter the circumstance, the Bible tells us clearly in Romans 8:28 that God will turn all situations around for good for those who love Him. When we stand on His Word and His promises, His goodness and His mercy will manifest in our lives!

So, for all those who have wondered these past decades if I blamed God for what happened to me, I can say emphatically, "No." Neither have I been angry at Him. I knew then, as I know now, He loves me with an everlasting love and His purposes for me are always good.

The next stop on my miracle road would take me to the windy city of Chicago. Well, after an important exercise in obedience. My faithful Heavenly Father wouldn't let me skip that essential step.

Healing in Forgiveness

"It takes a strong person to say they're sorry and an even stronger person to forgive."

- Yolanda Hadid

God had big plans to bring me through my physical recovery in a miraculous way. However, He was just as concerned about the hurt in my heart. I had some unfinished business to attend to. The underlying essence of the Bible is God's commitment to forgiveness. God sent His only Son to redeem sinful man so that we could live out the freedom of forgiveness. No human apart from Jesus lives a perfect life. Each of us needs God's forgiveness, and we're commanded to extend it to others. The scriptures are full of examples of how necessary forgiveness is. In fact, the term *forgive* is listed more than 60 times in some translations of the Bible.

Over two thousand years ago, when Jesus was asked by His disciples how many times they were required to forgive those who offended them, they were astounded by His answer. The religious leaders of that day taught that Jews were responsible to forgive a person three times, but on the fourth offense were no longer required to do so. So, imagine the apostle Peter's surprise when he asked Christ if he needed to forgive seven times (more than twice the Rabbinical expectation), and Jesus replied, "No, not seven times, but seventy times seven!"

Oh my, if we take Jesus' words literally, that means we need to be willing to forgive each other 490 times! If we even attempted to count each offense, as some may be tempted to, the burden of keeping a tally in a giant book would be too great. And, how about all the times we miss the mark regarding how God wants us to act? No, Jesus commands us to forgive more times than we can possibly track. Jesus told a parable to His followers about a servant who was forgiven much by a merciful king, only to turn around and withhold forgiveness from a friend who owed him little. Check out the story in the Gospel of Matthew, chapter 18, verses 21-35. How often do we forget just how much we have been forgiven by a Holy God, only to hold others' sins against them?

The day after the crash, when Steve (the driver who hit us) was bonded out of jail by his parents, he went directly to his pastor's home. Steve told preacher Kenneth Morris that he had done something very bad, which he felt very sorry about and was extremely regretful. Steve also said he knew he needed God and wanted to repent. Brother Kenneth prayed with him, and Steve asked Jesus to be his Savior that same day. I later learned that the severity of my injuries, coupled with the fact that I was his son's age, is what truly knocked him to his knees.

Soon after the crash Steve's parents came to see me in the hospital. They brought me a dozen long-stemmed, red roses, and said they were so sorry about what happened. After a few minutes, they mentioned their son. They told me Steve truly regretted what he had done and wanted to know if he could come see me as well. They shared that he was eager to apologize to me in person.

I didn't respond to that. I didn't know what to say. My parents didn't jump in and offer for him to visit. After a tense moment of silence as their request registered in our hearts, Dad addressed their concerns by saying, "He doesn't have to fear retaliation from us."

Later, when they left my room, I looked at Dad and said, "I don't think I can or want to see him."

After all, this was the man who changed my life in such a tragic way. I just wasn't ready to look him in the eyes. Dad told me it was understandable to feel that way, and I didn't have to see him if I didn't want to. He just reminded me not to let resentment take root in my heart. Dad talked again about Jesus not deserving what happened to Him and how He forgave those who crucified Him, praying "Father forgive them for they know not what they do."

Dad counseled me with the following, "Even though we don't understand why this happened, we need to forgive."

"I know," was my reply, looking down at my hands. "And, I do forgive him. It would just be really hard to see him right now."

I understood deep down that, in light of all that Jesus endured to pay for my sins, I was going to have to forgive Steve. In fact, if I didn't, my relationship with God would be negatively affected. Forgiveness is so important to God that Jesus taught about it right after modeling the Lord's Prayer in Matthew 6:14-15. In verse 15, He told His disciples, *"But if you do not forgive others their sins, your Father will not forgive your sins."* (NIV)

Ouch! Forgiveness is truly God's mandate. And I'm so grateful for the Lord's patience with me expressed through my Dad. He promptly went to the nurses' station and told them a man named Steve may try to come see me, but I wasn't ready for him to visit. The staff, always caring and protective of me, said they would keep that from happening. They posted a sign on my door that read "All visitors report to the nurse's station." That way, if Steve came to the hospital he would have to check in and they would turn him away.

A few days passed and visitors galore came to see me. I could have used a social secretary for sure! Then after several days, Dad insisted that Mom take a break from sitting in the hospital and he took her out to lunch. As I was talking with my sister and a friend, it occurred to me to ask the nurses to remove the sign. Why, at that point? I don't know, but God was up to something. When I told the nurse to take down the sign she asked if I was sure about that. I said I was. It just seemed so bothersome for all my family and friends to check in with them every time they came to spend time with me.

It seemed only minutes passed after I made that decision, when all of a sudden Brother Kenneth walked into my room. He was followed by Steve's parents and then Steve entered behind them. I didn't remember him from the crash since I was unconscious that night. Yet with his preacher and his parents present, I knew it was him. When he came into the room my eyes went straight to the wall in front of me. I couldn't look at him. He walked by the foot of my bed and stood on my left side. I didn't look over at him, just starred at the wall opposite me. I could feel heat creeping up my face and my sister said my face turned beet red. The only word I can use to explain my feelings in that moment is "violated." How could I look at him? When he spoke to me, my heart pounded in my chest.

"Angela, I'm sorry for what I did to you," Steve said. "I just want to know if you would forgive me."

When I opened my mouth to speak, still focusing all my attention on the wall, I heard myself say, "Yes." Though prior to his visit I had purposed in my heart to forgive him, it was in speaking it out loud that it really happened.

My visitors didn't stay long. The preacher prayed over me for my healing and then they left. As they were walking down the hallway, they ran into my parents. Dad told me about the encounter. He said that Steve had tears in his eyes and repeated, "I would never have purposely done that to Angela." Dad told him he knew that to be true, however, he had made two wrong choices the night of the crash. First, he chose to get drunk. Next, he chose to get behind the wheel of a car, taking a chance on his life and the lives of anyone else on the road. We were the ones affected. My life had been drastically changed. Nonetheless, each of us chose to forgive him.

When God is in the driver's seat of our lives, working everything out for our good and His Glory, nothing should surprise us. Who would have thought that the very day the nurses took away the sign requiring all visitors to check in, Steve was on his way to see me? By then I had realized how important forgiveness was to my emotional health. Though it would still take time for me to mend emotionally, saying "yes" to his plea and being willing to forgive, was as crucial for me as for him. I couldn't say another word to him that day, but I committed in my heart to forgive him. Steve, I honestly believe, had come to understand what a terrible choice he had made to drink and drive. Though he had driven drunk many times before, in confronting what he had done to me, he truly woke up to how serious the crime of drunk driving is, and how quickly it can destroy lives.

While I was still in the hospital, Steve was summoned to court. We were not notified when he appeared before the judge. Back in 1987, the laws about driving under the influence were not as strict as they are today, nor were victims' rights as big a deal. Steve opted for 45 days of rehabilitation, while I fought for over three months to be able to walk again. During those weeks he came back to the hospital several times.

One visit he sat and talked with my mom. During their conversation Mom admitted there had been a point when she had wished it was him laying in the hospital bed and not her firstborn daughter. In her transparent way, she shared a bit of the agony she had felt watching her child suffer. Then she did the unexpected. Mom asked Steve to forgive her for ever wishing such a thing. She told him she wanted a clean slate before God and had let go of any bitterness toward him. I believe her honesty, and forgiving heart, had a major impact on him.

Truly remorseful for the damage he had caused, Steve later asked Dad what he could to do to make up for his actions. How could he help us? Dad told him since he was responsible for the crash, he should pay my hospital bills. Steve agreed. This meant getting a job and not relying on the disability check he had been receiving for a back injury two years prior. So, Dad had papers drawn up and notarized. Every one of my bills during those first few months went straight to him. We never paid a penny of it.

Steve's willingness to take responsibility for the crash that changed my life made it easier for me to forgive him. But it was still a journey. Over the past decades I've learned a lot about how forgiveness works in our lives, what it looks like. True forgiveness is a decision not to hold another's sin against them: to not bring it up, and to leave it with God, covered by His grace. Forgiveness doesn't exempt the offender from the wrong doing or let them off the hook in regards to the consequences of their actions. It doesn't mean being best friends or even the assurance of an ongoing relationship. It is an act of the will that sets the one offended free. Truly, I could talk to Steve face-to-face today without any bitterness or resentment in my heart because I turned it over to God long ago. God took it then and continued the healing in my heart and body. Once again, He proved His commands to be essential for healthy living:

"...bearing with one another, and forgiving one another, if anyone has a complaint against another; even as Christ forgave you, so you also must do. But above all these things put on love, which is the bond of perfection. And let the peace of God rule in your hearts, to which also you were called in one body; and be thankful"

Colossians 3:13-15 (NKJV).

Now I was ready for God's next steps in my recovery. Some big strides indeed.

ANGELA ADKINS

Big City Strides

"Toto, I've a feeling we're not in Kansas anymore!"
Dorothy in *The Wizard of Oz*

Five weeks of hospitalization is a long time for any 15-year-old, especially for one trying so desperately to walk again. As I worked with my care givers, giving my best in physical therapy, it was evident I needed more intensive rehabilitation to cope with my disability. The Forest General staff discussed my options with my parents. Dad was informed the cost of local rehabilitation centers was upwards of $600 per day! Of course, this seemed an insurmountable expense on a preacher's salary, so we prayed for God's intervention.

Our hospital case worker, who had become very dear to us, suggested we inquire about the Shriners and their services for children. Soon, three Shriners came to visit me. Standing by my bedside, one of the gentlemen teared up. "Angela, we want to do everything we can to help you," he said.

Despite their sincere compassion for my situation, they were unable to promise me anything. In fact, they shared there was a long wait for new patients to be admitted to one of their facilities, sometimes up to a year before a bed would be available. Still, they would check for me and see how else they could be of help in the meantime. Again, God surrounded me with thoughtful people with big hearts.

When the Almighty directs our steps, people respond with awe. Everyone was amazed when the Shriners returned for a second visit with great news! A hospital bed in their Chicago facility had become immediately available for a new patient; something we were told had never happened before. We knew it was another miracle and that God had made a way where there seemed to be no way. Additionally, a Shriner who lived elsewhere in Mississippi owned a private plane and was willing to transport me to the Chicago hospital.

It was mid-November when Forest General Hospital began my transfer paperwork, attending to all the details of my relocation to the Shriners Children's Hospital in Chicago., I'll never forget my excitement when the ambulance came to take me to the small airport for my first airplane ride. Though the helicopter ride on the night of the crash was a lost memory, this trip was full of hope! Then we noticed the narrow, metal gurney I was to lay on for the long trip across country.

"That just won't do," was the immediate reaction of the nurses. Dad agreed that the gurney looked way too uncomfortable. The staff bustled about in search of foam mattress covers and extra blankets to make me a suitable travel bed. Once I was all wrapped up, as comfortable as I could be, the nurses gave the okay for the paramedics to take me. With so much excitement swirling in the air, any sadness at leaving "home base" was diminished. Everyone wished me well. Hope in God's best outcome was contagious.

The ambulance arrived at the air strip and then drove me right up to the plane. What a blessing to be able to use a small plane at a small airport. Someone had alerted the local television station and newspaper because they were present to see me off. Perhaps it was the Shriners who called them; we never knew for sure. The result was my friends saw me on television and read about me in the paper, this time with much better news than before. Once onboard, I received farewell hugs and kisses from Dad and Renea as they couldn't go with us. Tears flowed, and we said our "See-you-laters."

Despite all the logistics and emotion of this trip, I marveled at the sheer adventure. My heart filled with gratitude because Mom was going with me. After she settled into the seat beside me, she handed me a mirror with a long handle. Why, you may ask. Well, since I was flat on my back for the whole trip unable to see the sky or land as we soared through the air, the mirror made it possible for me to appreciate the beautiful sights. By holding it up to the window and angling it just so, I could view the changing landscape below and the awesome cloud formations too. At such a high altitude God's creation is truly breathtaking! My mom even took pictures from her seat.

The flight from Hattiesburg to Chicago, roughly 829 miles due north, took us nearly eight hours in that little prop plane. Even though the nurses had me cushioned very well, I could feel the vibration of the plane the whole trip. We made a pit stop in Paducah, Kentucky, to refuel, get drinks, etc., then back into the air we went. As we arrived in Chicago that night, the city lights reflected in my mirror were amazing! I felt like Alice taking a trip to Wonderland, or Dorothy landing in Oz. Having lived in rural towns and smaller cities all my life, nothing prepared me for the vastness of the Chicago skyline. It truly looked like another world to me.

Even after we landed, I could feel the vibration of the airplane in my body. This sensation lasted during the ambulance ride to the hospital and throughout the rest of the night. I shared with Mom how weird it was to still feel like I was on the plane. Folks who continue to feel the motion of a cruise liner, even weeks after they return home, will appreciate how odd the sensation was. However, it didn't diminish the joy of our trip and the many pleasant memories I treasure.

The hospital, a state-of-the-art Shriner facility, is definitely geared for children. The hospital staff was very welcoming. They went above and beyond to get me settled in for the night. I remember the whole building was designed with vibrant colors: from the walls, the décor, and the curtains that went around each patient's bed. My room had four beds in it, with curtains that could be drawn around each one for privacy when we dressed or rested. Parents had separate rooms and Mom said hers was just like being in a hotel. Of course, she was with me most of the time and only used her room to sleep. There was also a social area called The Mall, where kids could hang out and have fun between their therapy sessions. Amenities included a mini basketball court, ping pong tables, a place to watch movies, and a table for a pizza party. My favorite detail in The Mall was the baby grand piano!

The first morning of my Chicago adventure began a full day of processing and orientation which included blood work, X-rays, and introductions to staff and fellow patients. The very next day when my therapy started, they needed my input regarding a custom wheelchair. What a blessing the Shriners are to families! They provide everything a patient needs from medical care, therapy, medical supplies and medical equipment. Since purple was my favorite color, my wheelchair would be purple and black. It was a very pricy order, something we could never have purchased. Though I needed it right then, I knew it wouldn't be for very long because I had faith I would walk again. While I pondered this in my heart, Mom was vocal about it. As the therapists placed the order, she flat out told them, "You are wasting your money. My daughter isn't going to need that wheelchair long." What Mom spoke out in faith, God was accomplishing!

During this season at the Children's Hospital, I would have two different therapies: physical and occupational. The physical therapy worked my legs, with the goal of getting them moving again. By now, feeling had returned to my ankles, but my feet felt like plastic. Hot and cold were unusual sensations. I still could not move my legs on my own, so therapy involved leg raises done by therapists who lifted my legs at different angles to work my muscles. Also, I was unable to hold myself up on the parallel bars yet, and I continued to wear the back brace given to me at Forest General after my back surgery. I had been told I would need to wear it when sitting for at least a year; however, I wore it for only nine months.

The goal of occupational therapy was to help me be as independent as possible. Among other things, I so appreciated how they taught me to use a sliding board so I could maneuver from the bed to the wheelchair on my own. During my time in Chicago, my school back home arranged for a tutor to help me stay current with my studies. Weeks passed quickly with days filled with therapy sessions and school work. Miraculously, when my hospital stays finished and I returned to school, I passed the 10th grade with my classmates!

In fact, during these long months in the hospital, the staff gave me a couple of nicknames. One was "Miracle Girl," because they saw things happening they couldn't explain. The other was "Tiger," because of the determination I showed in therapy. I just wasn't going to give up, and nothing was going to stop me. Truly, I believe that God was giving me an inner strength I wouldn't have had if there hadn't been so many people praying for me.

God's continued provision astounded us. For instance, my parents had friends who had relocated to the suburbs of Chicago years before the crash. Wouldn't you know they became an important support for Mom and me. They were delighted to show us around the city and even hosted us in their home when the hospital let me have some weekend breaks. I remember my fascination with the skyscrapers, because true to their name, I could not see the tops of them as we drove by. Also, I learned that the nickname Windy City was perfect for Chicago. It was cold and very windy that time of year. In fact, the city was blanketed by a blizzard in 1987, a sight I couldn't have imagined.

On the night it happened, the nurses figured snow wasn't something this Southern girl was familiar with. Indeed, as everyone talked about the coming storm I couldn't comprehend what a blizzard might look like, or the amount of snow that could accumulate. Actually, I doubted I'd see any snow at all. Hours after all us kids were sound asleep, the blizzard began silently. It was around midnight when a nurse came to my room and awakened me. Then she pulled open the window curtain and said, "Angela, look outside!" I opened my eyes to see white wind blowing in every direction. The snow was coming down so hard and was already sticking to the ground. It looked like a severe thunderstorm, but instead of rain it was snow.

"WOW! That's so cool!" was all I could say. With the majesty of nature swirling around our building I don't know how I managed to fall back to sleep. Early the next morning Mom came into the room with news of the snow. "Is it still out there?" I asked.

In Mississippi a flurry of tiny snow crystals was a very rare occurrence, and if they did make it to the ground, they were gone within moments. Yet, here in Chicago, Mom responded, "It sure is! Look!" as she pulled back the curtains to show me. At least a foot of snow covered the ground, and I so wanted to go outside to experience the wonderland. The nurse allowed us to make a short visit outside, directing us to "Bundle up! It's 40 below zero."

"What?!" I thought, and then quickly discovered how the wind outside sliced right through us. After all the effort of layering up to protect us from the cold, we only lasted a few minutes outside. Though I loved the snow, I was ready to get back inside and admire it from the window!

Part Three

Healing Miracles

"Where there is hope, there is faith. Where there is faith, miracles happen!"

Anonymous

The intensive physical therapy I had received at the hospital really paid off. One week after my arrival in Chicago, I was not only able to get up from my bed and transfer to a wheelchair all by myself, but I could also spend the whole day sitting up! A lot of people take sitting up for granted, but not me. When I remember how I couldn't tolerate being out of bed for more than an hour while recuperating in Mississippi, I realize just how momentous my improvement had been. Indeed, I progressed rapidly. As my pelvis healed, my legs strengthened, and the staff started working with me on the parallel bars. My therapy sessions lasted for hours each day, and I dove into the challenge for four weeks straight.

Some folks wondered what was the key to my success. Aside from bubble gum bubbles, I'm sure it boiled down to faith, attitude and miracles. As you've seen through the first part of my journey, my family's faith in God's all-powerful ability to heal me was essential in trusting Him for what we couldn't see. The Bible says in Hebrews 11:1, "Now faith is the substance of things hoped for, the evidence of things not seen." Since God has given us mighty promises to stand on in His Word, we could have faith He was able to do what we could not do for ourselves.

What I could control was my attitude, and it's very important we cooperate with God as we trust Him. So, I approached therapy with a commitment never to say, "I can't." Instead, I determined to answer anything they asked me to do with, "I'll try." This was a decision based on good advice from friends back home in Mississippi. They told me before I left for Chicago that if I'd set my mind to accomplishing everything expected of me, I'd probably come home sooner. With that resolve I felt God with me, helping me push a little bit further every day. My progress continued on the parallel bars as I got stronger and I rejoiced. Then I mastered the ability to swing my legs while sitting on a bench. However, I still couldn't move them in any other direction.

God is the One who was healing my body and giving me the strength to carry on. I knew His plans for me were for good, and even more than I could imagine. The apostle Paul wrote in the third chapter of his letter to the Ephesian church the following: *"Now to him who is able to do immeasurably more than all we ask or imagine, according to his power that is at work within us..."*

Ephesians 3:20

One particular evening when I experienced God's miraculous touch will always shine like the north star in my memory. After a busy day, all my roommates and I were tucked in for the night. I was laying on my side, my usual position, with a pillow between my legs placed there by the nurses. This had been the norm from the start. The staff always had an extra sheet under me so that when I got uncomfortable, since I couldn't move myself, they could draw up the sheet, helping me to roll over. For some reason I wasn't particularly tired that night; in fact, I felt a stirring of anticipation. Since I had been praying, along with a multitude of others, for my legs to move, I suddenly had an urge to test what they could do. So, I looked down at my legs, curled in a fetal position, and under my breath I spoke words of faith to them.

Jesus taught His followers about the faith they should have by saying, "For assuredly, I say to you, whoever says to this mountain, 'Be removed and be cast into the sea,' and does not doubt in his heart, but believes that those things he says will be done, he will have whatever he says. *Therefore, I say to you, whatever things you ask when you pray, believe that you receive them, and you will have them*"

Mark 11:23-24

In my heart I simply felt it was time for my legs to move. Looking down at them, I whispered so as not to disturb the other patients, "Move!! Just move!!" I repeated this numerous times while I tried to straighten my legs with everything I had in me. Sure enough, as I spoke it and believed it would happen, my legs moved. They straightened out! I was overjoyed!

Ok, I thought. Pulling them back up into a curled position, I said, "Legs move!" How many times I moved my legs up and down that evening, I can't tell you. I was ecstatic! Finally, as I thanked God for answering all the prayers offered up on my behalf, I fell into a contented sleep. The next morning when Mom came into my room, imagine my excitement. I flipped my covers back and I said, "Look Mom!" She beamed with thanksgiving as I proceeded to move my legs up and down like I had the night before. It was the first time since the crash I could do that. Of course, we couldn't wait to call Dad with the news. I was progressing on my miracle road and giving God all the glory.

As time went on, I went from the wheelchair, to a walker, and eventually to loft strand crutches that attach to my forearms. I had reached a point the doctors thought was impossible. But God! While the doctors and nurses marveled at my improvement, I pondered what Jesus had taught, *"With men this is impossible, but with God all things are possible."*

Matthew 19:26

Truly, nothing is impossible for our Almighty God! The victory I experienced in moving my legs caused me to be bold about other deep desires I had. I shared with Mom how I was determined to get my driver's license and drive a car without hand controls, and to be able to play the piano while pressing down on the pedals. I committed to pray for these desires, so close to my heart, in Jesus' name.

Just prior to the crash, my favorite class at school had been driver's education. I already had my learner's permit and was only 12 days away from getting my license that October. Driving a car had fascinated me since I was little. Sitting up front, next to my parents on the bench seat (in the days before child restraints and car seats), they would allow me to put my little hand on the wheel and pretend I was driving. Because of my serious attitude, after some time they let me control more of the wheel, always steadying it and keeping us safe. I felt so grown up! Later, when I was a young teenager, both Dad and Mom taught me how to drive on the back roads. Since in Mississippi one could get a learner's permit at 14, lots of the kids my age were gleaning experience from their folks.

It was a memorable day in my 10th grade driver's ed class when it was my turn to practice driving around cones and perfecting my ability to maneuver the vehicle. As usual, there were four of us students accompanied by the coach who sat up front with dual controls. Coach gave me some great pointers that day, and I was really enjoying the class until it was time for the one student without any experience to get behind the wheel. Just like in a scene from a movie, the three of us more experienced drivers buckled up in the backseat and tried not to be nervous. The coach was patient to walk our peer through every step. Funny, I don't remember much about her driving around the cones. In fact I think she hit just about every one. What was truly frightening was that when it came time for her to make a turn to either the right or left, she didn't change course. Despite the coach's gentle prompts, she just kept driving straight forward toward the fence in front of us. Finally his voice became stern, as the three of us in the back went from wide-eyed to screaming loudly because the fence loomed close! Thank God the coach took over, braking from his set of controls and steered us to safety. Even so, I was eager to drive again.

How like that coach is our Father God! He is patient with us, instructing us in the ways we should go, how we are to think, and act. Then sometimes when life gets completely out of control, He calmly steps in and handles the situation. In the beginning of my recovery, my great desire to drive seemed like a lost privilege. But I'm a fighter, not a quitter. I began to earnestly pray that God would enable me to accomplish this.

As I regained feeling in my legs and began to move them on my own, I had yet to sense any normal feeling in my feet. Actually, the best I could describe them at that point was to say my feet felt like plastic. I couldn't move them at all. The muscles in my ankles were weak as well, affecting my balance. Still, the doctors were astonished that I had regained all the feeling from my waist down to my ankles. They would say, "It's amazing!" Or, "It's phenomenal!" No one could explain my miraculous progress. They just encouraged me with, "Keep it up!"

Of course, my parents and I knew my recovery was due to answered prayers. Jesus, our Healer, was working in my life. The blood He shed for my healing was working one miraculous occurrence after another.

About that time, there was a day Mom and I were sitting close to the baby grand piano in the mall area of the hospital. I reminded her of my desire to play again with the ability to depress the sustain petal without problems. We committed to pray for this and within days, as my therapy continued, my right foot regained some movement! I couldn't move my feet from side to side but I began to be able to press my right foot down and back up. Though my left foot still didn't move, the range of motion in my right one was just enough to meet my prayer request.

I was only fifteen years old and didn't fully understand the power of the spoken word. Now I've learned a lot more about the importance of the Word of God and how His truth works in our lives. When I spoke out in faith, He began accomplishing miracles. The Bible says, *"Death and life are in the power of the tongue, and those who love it will eat its fruit."*

Proverbs 18:21

And from the Book of Deuteronomy, *"I have set before you life and death, blessing and cursing; therefore choose life, that both you and your descendants may live; that you may love the LORD your God, that you may obey His voice, and that you may cling to Him, for He is your life and the length of your days..."*

Deuteronomy 30:19-20

As far as our requests of God, Philippians 4:6 states, "Be anxious for nothing, but in everything by prayer and supplication, with thanksgiving, let your requests be made known to God." And from 1 John 5:15, "And if we know that He hears us, whatever we ask, we know that we have the petitions that we have asked of Him."

As we can see in the Word, God tells us to speak and make our requests known to Him. We are to speak life and choose blessings. He gives us free will to choose what we speak and what we will stand on, showing us the life of Jesus Christ, our precious Lord and Savior, as an example. Study the gospels, the life of Jesus and the instructions He gave us. He went to the cross to redeem us and put us in right standing with the Father. Those who believe in Him are saved. In Matthew 16:19 (NKJV), Jesus said to Peter regarding the church (God's people, the body of Christ), "And I will give you the keys of the kingdom of heaven, and whatever you bind on earth will be bound in heaven, and whatever you loose on earth will be loosed in heaven." He gave us authority in His name. We can speak according to His Word, and He will bring it to pass when we believe.

Once my right foot began to move, Mom got me over to the piano, encouraging me to practice. I remember it was difficult at first because of how different my foot felt, but it began to work well. Then, when I got out of the hospital she took me out on country roads and said, "It's time to practice!" Before I knew it, I was driving the car again. I passed my driving test and received my driver's license shortly afterwards!

What I know now, that I didn't fully grasp then, is the concept of how speaking to your mountain as Jesus told us to, works. God honored my requests because I had the belief and determination in faith that He would do it. Now I look back and see how He was working all things together for my good. I focus on the importance of what Jesus said in Mark 11:24, that when you pray, believe that you receive, and you will have what you pray for. He didn't say "maybe"; but you will have it!

The Great Physician

"Faith changes hope into reality."

Kenneth E. Hagen

Then I had a set-back.

Now, everyone experiences set-backs in this life. Some are financial, some are emotional and some are physical; some are brief and some are life-altering. The thing is, often there is little warning before a set-back strikes. I've come to see such critical times as opportunities for God to shine through our trials. He gets a lot of glory by stepping in and turning set-backs around. Amen?

Christmas 1987 was fast approaching and the medical staff made plans to let me go home for a short break. It had been since Thanksgiving that I had seen Dad and Renea. As incredible as it seemed, I had not been home since the crash! How I looked forward to spending time with family and friends! My heart yearned to enjoy a little "normalcy." Even knowing I had to return to the hospital after Christmas, my spirit danced at the opportunity to go home.

The doctors were very pleased with my progress, so I brought up the issue of my back brace. At that point I so hoped I could stop using it. The brace was such a pain to have to wrap before every shower, let alone putting it on when I got out of bed, and taking it off when I went to lay down. Pondering my request, the doctor said he needed to run some tests to see how my spine was healing before I could be free of it. Then we'd know better after I returned from my break.

The test (called a Myelogram) involved injecting dye into my spine to get a clear picture of my spinal cord. It was rough. I had a reaction to the dye and got very sick. The dye gave me a bad headache, prompted a fever, and caused me to be nauseous with an upset stomach. At one point my fever climbed so high, the staff had to strip me down and cram ice packs all around me to bring it down. Still, God brought me through the ordeal, restoring my health. Finally, preparations were made to release me for Christmas break. I wouldn't learn the results of the scan until I returned to Chicago after the holidays.

After a sweet time back home, I fully expected to be freed from the brace. It functioned much like a cast, holding me in the proper position until my back could completely heal. Enthusiastic about all the ground I had covered in therapy and my renewed strength, I was definitely unprepared for the results of the test. In fact, you could say I was completely blind-sided.

The myelogram showed my back was collapsing. On top of that I was told that the surgery done in Mississippi was done incorrectly. The chief surgeon at Shriner's said the test showed a bone graft only on one side of my spine instead of on both sides, like it should have been. He said, in fact, there was bone missing. This of course we already knew about because the doctor in Mississippi had told us he needed to remove a crushed vertebrae, yet we had assumed it had been corrected with the bone graft. The surgeon proceeded to tell me that if my back kept moving the way it was, the rods would snap, break through my skin, and I would once again be paralyzed. Oh my! After all my hard work in physical therapy, I couldn't imagine starting at the beginning again. This was devastating news.

"The only answer to this problem," the surgeon said, "is to open your back again, take the rods out, and put smaller ones in." He also wanted to scrape more bone off my hip and take a rib, in order to do proper bone grafts on my spine. Having laid out his professional plan of attack, he left the room. In the wake of his departure, his horrific prognosis hung in the air and I felt despair overwhelm me. Emotionally, I plummeted to rock bottom. For me, that was the hardest day I faced throughout the whole ordeal of the crash. I began to sob.

All Mom could do at that moment was hold me while I cried my heart out. Her tears mingled with mine as we both "doggie paddled" in what seemed to be an endless ocean of grief. How I needed the steadying arm of my Savior. God saw and knew just what I was feeling. He had His own plan about what should happen next, because He is the great physician.

When my sobs dwindled to whimpers and my bed was littered with Kleenex, I gathered my thoughts and decided to call Dad. While I depended on Mom to pray for me and tend to my physical needs, I knew Dad always had encouraging words to give me peace and calm. Oh, how I thank God for my precious parents! I love them dearly and admire them greatly. Since my sister and I are extremely close, I knew the whole family would ache for me in view of this set-back.

On hearing my report of the doctor's prognosis, Dad immediately reminded me that I should not be afraid. He told me God could heal me completely and there would never have to be another knife touching my back except to remove the rods that were already there. Or, if God chose to work through an additional surgery, He would bring me through just like he did before. As we continued to talk, Dad's words based on scripture calmed me down, and I felt the peace of God surround me again. I would trust that my Heavenly Father had everything under control and I was going to be all right.

Before we hung up, Dad asked me to have the doctor call him. When they spoke, Dad heard the exact diagnosis I had been given, and requested a written report be mailed to him as well. The doctor sent Dad a detailed letter about my situation and suggested I go home for a couple of weeks. He said he wanted Dad to come back with me when I returned so they could further discuss the issue with my spine and plan the surgery.

While I was home, we attended a revival meeting at a church in Ellisville, Mississippi. Revivals are special times of ministry when God's people focus on repenting from sin, glorifying God and receiving His powerful blessings. I had always enjoyed such times of deep worship with my sisters and brothers in Christ. That night, as soon as I went into the church, I could feel the presence of the Lord and the love of His people. At that point I was still in a wheelchair, but learning to walk more and more with my crutches.

As the service was drawing to a close, Dad pushed me up front to be prayed for during the altar call time. Several young people gathered around me as we prayed. They took my hands, lifting me up and started walking me all around the front of the church and then around the pulpit. One of my best friends was pointing at my side, crying, "Jesus! Jesus!" After service was over, Dad stood up in front of everyone and said, "As you were praying for Angela, God showed me an X-ray vision of her back. I saw that missing bone going into her spine, right back into place. God made her back, and he can certainly put bone where there needs to be bone." Hallelujah!

When the day came to head back to Chicago, my heart began to pound. On the plane I told Dad I didn't want to sit and hear the doctors describe my back in detail again. I wondered if there was any way Dad could speak to them without me present. Upon arriving at the hospital, the staff took me directly for more X-rays. Then they put Dad and me in a room to wait for the doctor. That's when Dad explained to the nurse that I preferred he speak to the doctor alone regarding my X-rays and any possible surgery. She said that would be fine. While I was laying on the table, Dad was sitting in a chair across from me with a view out into the hallway. He watched the doctor take my X-rays into the room right across the hall and put them on the lighted board to view.

My father didn't share with me at the moment what he witnessed going on, even though it amazed him. He saw the doctor look at the X-Rays, then go from one side to the other, tilting his head with a puzzled expression on his face. Later Dad told me it seemed the doctor looked at the X-rays from every possible angle, except for standing on his head! Then he exited the room, only to return with another doctor. Moments later, another doctor joined them. Before he knew it, the room was full of doctors puzzling over my X-rays. Finally, the nurse came over to us and informed Dad the doctor was ready to talk to him.

When Dad walked into the room, the doctor reiterated that a few weeks prior he had notified him I needed surgery on my back. Dad acknowledged that he knew this to be the doctor's prognosis. "Well," continued the doctor, "surgery is not necessary now."

Dad, knowing that God had healed me, just had to ask him, "What about that bone you said is missing?"

His only response was, "Um....it's there now!" He then pointed to the old X-rays where the bone was clearly missing, comparing them to the new x-rays that showed new bone. In fact, the doctor pointed out I now had bone graft on both sides of my spine, whereas before I did not. He then declared my back looked great and was healing nicely. There was no room at all for doubt.

The nurse was just as excited as everybody else. She rushed into the room where I was waiting and with a big smile said, "I'm going to let your dad tell you the good news."

"What good news?" I asked, though by that point I was grinning from ear to ear too. I could feel my whole body tremble with joy. She grinned widely and exited just minutes before Dad joined me. As I lay there I started to repeat to myself, "Good News? Good News!" Tears sprang to my eyes as I began thanking God for all He had done. In those brief moments, pure joy at my Savior's loving care flooded me. Before Dad even told me the results of the X-rays, I had a deep assurance in my heart that God had healed me and I was NOT going to have more surgery. Still, it was really exciting to hear all these details.

The purpose driving the writing of this book is to share two very important things about God: He can't lie and He can't fail. His Word confirms that He loves humanity beyond measure. Those who humbly receive the gift of salvation, and follow Jesus Christ as Redeemer, experience God's healing touch in miraculous ways.

I can testify that I experienced promise after promise through His Word while I was in the hospital. I received many miracles, one after the other during the three months of my recovery. God brought me through and I'm truly thankful to Him!

It wouldn't be until three years after the crash that another knife touched my back. In December, 1990, I returned to the Shriner Hospital in Philadelphia, where I had been doing my follow-up appointments. The reason for this visit was to finally remove the Harrington rods, which doctors felt unnecessary after so much time. As a precaution, however, the surgeon had Dad sign papers consenting to additional rods or bone grafting if my spine needed them. After surgery, while still in recovery, my first question was, "Did they have to put more rods in?"

"No," said the doctor, "All we did was remove the old rods, nothing else needed to be done." Then he said my back looked great, the bone graft had healed nicely, and I was doing just fine. Yet another confirmation that God had done the work!

It's hard to believe this was over thirty years ago. You see, what I went through I would never wish on anyone, not even my worst enemy. I remember nights being awakened by a nurse because she heard me crying in my sleep. Even the sleeping pills they gave me for a short time couldn't suppress the torturous pain I felt. Many nights I would awaken to feel tears rolling down my face from trying to move my legs and not being able to. It was truly a nightmare for a very active teen with big dreams like me. Despite the wonderful assessment by the surgeon the day the rods came out, it still seemed my childhood dreams to become an actress or a model were lost forever.

Then God took this very bad thing and turned it around for good.

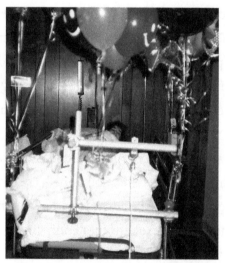

I was in the hospital bed here with so many balloons they joked that my bed would fly away. Family, friends, and the community showered me with so many gifts. I felt very loved and knew that many were praying for me.

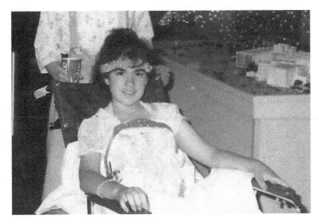

I was in a wheelchair with a back brace on in the hospital lobby. I was still in a lot of pain here. The headband was a gift from one of the sweet nurses that took care of me.

Beyond doctors' expectations, I started walking with forearm crutches. Amazed medical staff called me "Miracle Girl."

God's Dreams for Me

"Happiness…consists in giving, and in serving others."
Henry Dummond

The very day we received the awesome report of how God healed my back, I was discharged from Shriner's. Now, my life could get back on track. Despite the doctors' expectations that I would be a paraplegic, dependent on a wheelchair with little (if any) use of my legs, I could WALK with the assistance of forearm crutches. By this point, I had total feeling and movement in my legs, except for the muscles in my ankles, which sometimes effected my balance. By God's mercy, my two main desires were fulfilled: I was able to drive a car without hand controls and I could press the sustain pedal when I played the piano. Thanks to Jesus, I found a way to accomplish everything that was important to me.

But what about my dreams to perform or pursue a modeling career? Had they been dashed for good in the blink of an eye on that dark country road five months earlier? Could God still use my outgoing personality and my desire to shine for Him in some big way? Hope began to penetrate my heart as I lay in the hospital those last few days. Even as I had talked to my legs, commanding them to move, I now heard myself say, "One day I'm going to have a story to tell."

During the summer months before my senior year in high school, just when I was fairly comfortable with the new "normal," my family moved from Mississippi to Maryland. It was 1989, and Dad took a pastoral position in a church in Salisbury, Maryland. That move was rough for me. For two weeks I cried myself to sleep and ate very little, skirting depression. The emotional upheaval of leaving my boyfriend and so many peers who had supported me during my recovery, was finally lessened as I made new friendships. Soon my joy for life returned and dreams to do something important with my life began to grow.

I believe God puts deep desires in our hearts for a reason. He gives us free will to choose which direction we'll go with those dreams and desires. His ultimate goal, however, is to share His grace through us, reaching others with the truth about salvation in Christ Jesus, all for His glory.

Three years after that move, in 1992, I felt a nudge. The thought occurred to me that a commercial about drunk driving, one that depicted the dangers inherent with driving under the influence, might benefit the community. I was only 20 years old when I first contacted a local news station in Maryland. A media staff member suggested I contact Mothers Against Drunk Driving (MADD) with my idea. I knew little about their organization and how they desire to promote healing and make a difference in the lives of others. When I called the local chapter, I was invited to a meeting where I could learn more about them and discuss how to get involved.

MADD is an organization with a four-fold mission. They exist to: end drunk driving; help fight drugged driving; support the victims of these violent crimes; and prevent underage drinking. Americans are impacted by drunk driving every day, especially because we spend significantly more time on the road than citizens of other countries. At the time of the writing of this book, these are the harrowing statistics taken from their website (*www.madd.org*): Every two minutes someone is injured in a drunk driving crash. Every 51 minutes someone is killed in a drunk driving crash. Two out of every three people will be impacted by a drunk driving crash in their lifetimes. However, since 1980 when MADD was founded, drunk driving deaths have decreased by 50 percent! More than 370,000 lives have been saved, and 840,000 people have been compassionately served by MADD representatives. This organization is the real deal and the work they do is phenomenal. When I got involved and began to learn how passionate MADD is about saving lives, I jumped in with both feet to help make a difference.

After meeting me, the president of our local MADD chapter started planning a public service announcement (PSA) to air on our local television stations. I was the one speaking on the PSA. It aired between tv shows and commercials, catching the attention of the Highway Safety program. They called and wanted me to do a PSA for them as well. I was delighted to help! As I shared my story with the MADD Victim support group, growing in my communication skills, an invitation came to speak on Victim Impact Panels. The VIP (as it is called) was a panel of victims, usually myself and one or two other folks who addressed first-time offenders. People charged with a DUI were required to pay fines, have their license revoked, and then sit and listen to victims describe the possible consequences involved with the criminal choice to drink and drive. The response was amazing. I lost count of the numerous times someone told me how much my story impacted them, causing them to vow never to drink and drive again!

In fact, I remember a day I was at a restaurant in Franklin, Tennessee, and noticed a man staring at me. I glanced over my shoulder to see if he was looking at someone behind me, but then he got up and began walking towards me. Not sure what was going on, I was relieved when he addressed me by name as he approached my table.

"Angela," he said, "I know you don't know who I am, but I was at one of the Victim Impact Panels you spoke at for MADD." The stranger shifted his weight and looked me straight in the eye. "I just want you to know your story really affected me. I will never drink and drive again. Thank you for sharing your story."

I smiled gratefully and replied, "Thank you so much! I'm so glad to hear that. It means a lot to me that I could help." As he walked away grinning, I couldn't help but praise God for using my story to touch his life in such a positive way. Though I'd often battle nervousness before sharing my testimony, it was all worth it. All my preparation and prayer paid off to know that lives were changed and someone would be spared the terrible tragedy I had endured.

After I moved to Tennessee in 1997, the local chapter of MADD in that state started booking me to speak in jails. I began addressing folks recently arrested for DUIs, those who would be in jail for varying lengths of time. This step-up was a real challenge for me. Prior to speaking at the VIP forums, I had experienced nervousness like "butterflies" in my stomach. When it came to going into jail and speaking to incarcerated offenders, my butterflies turned into "man-eating moths!" There were times before I went to speak, I'd sit on the floor in the middle of my bedroom, rocking back and forth, holding my stomach and crying, "I don't want to do this."

Looking back, I think this was so difficult at first, because by going into the jails the devastation caused by offenders was so real. Though I had forgiven Steve, the offender who caused our crash, I was still healing emotionally and physically. Yet, every time I pushed through my emotional turmoil and went to speak in the jail, the results were incredible and God-breathed. The feedback from the offenders affirmed my story was changing their lives. By the end of each event, after reliving my ordeal again, I would breathe a sigh of relief knowing my gut-wrenching struggle was really worth it.

Of the many stories I could share, one in particular stands out. It happened when I went to speak at the women's jail. Now, God tells us to go minister to the prisoner. His Spirit gives us love for those who are incarcerated, and compassion for those serving time. Still, it was a very sobering experience. Picture the razor wire surrounding the building, the stark walls and the heavy metal doors. Visitors are asked to leave all jewelry and personal items in their cars or in a locker before being processed to enter the room where the inmates will be. There are alarms on the doors and loud clicks as you progress down the hallway, all of which can be unnerving as you enter a guarded environment so foreign from every day experience.

As I neared the end of my talk that day, a lady began to sob loudly. Several inmates stood to comment as I finished, and this woman stood as well, with tears streaming from her face. Her words were barely audible, chocked off by racking cries. Somehow she managed to communicate that she was in jail for a DUI. Her victim was 14 years old, the same age I was when I was struck by a drunk driver. The teen had died. The family was devastated. Then, as her sobs subsided for just a moment, she asked in a trembling voice, "I just want to know if you will forgive me."

It was a holy moment. God was in that room. This woman I had never met and would most likely never see again, had just laid bare her soul. She needed to hear that someone would forgive her, and that she was redeemable. I spoke to her with gentle words, trying to lift her up. In no way did I imply her DUI actions were okay, but I told her she could be forgiven by God and that I, too, forgave her. Sitting back down, she continued to bawl like a baby.

Within minutes the other prisoners filed out of the room, and a counselor was summoned to talk to this woman. The facilitator of the meeting approached me and informed me that this lady had been denying the severity of her crime ever since she arrived. She had been a problem prisoner, rebelling against the rules, acting out her guilt and anger, starting fights. No one had been able to reach her, so her reaction to my story was surprising. The reality of how drunk driving affected my life broke through her denial, and the facilitator felt the counselor would finally be able to work with her. As hard as it was to witness this inmate's distress, I knew God was at work in that situation. I thanked Him yet again for using my story to make a change in her life for the better.

Not only was God fulfilling my dream of making a difference, but He always showed His tender care for me personally. There came a time during my ministry when I was asked if I had spoken with the man who had caused the crash that changed my life, and, did I know how he was doing. I realized it would be important for me to make contact with Steve. As I've said, I had forgiven him. If our paths crossed today, I could look him straight in the eyes and tell him honestly I hold nothing against him. Yet, back then, it seemed necessary to reach out so I could be certain my involvement in MADD was not against him as an individual, but rather my stand against the dangerous and criminal act of drunk driving.

You can imagine how my heart pounded the day I dialed his number. I didn't want Steve to think I was calling to harass him. I just wanted to know how he was doing. When he answered the phone, and I identified myself, I could hear a catch in his voice. He told me he was glad I called and asked how my family and I were doing. He seemed genuinely interested in how I was, just as I was interested in him. I told him about my involvement with MADD, to which he responded he was pleased that I was doing so well. That was it. As I hung up the receiver, I grinned because I knew my heart was truly clear of any residual bitterness.

I haven't talked to him since, but I believe that short call was another necessary step in my healing process. Prior to this, the only word I had spoken to him was "yes" when he first asked me to forgive him. It was my ministry to others that inspired me to reach out to the one who had caused me so much pain. Since I knew he was truly sorry, I felt compelled to let him know I had honestly forgiven him. I expect Steve will always remember me, but more importantly, I pray he will always remember what God has done for all of us.

God took the tragic crash I experienced and used it for me to offer healing to others. I couldn't help but sense my dreams and desires were becoming more real than they had ever been before.

In His Service

"I don't know what your destiny will be. But one thing I do know: the only ones among you who will be really happy are those who sought and found how to serve."

— Albert Schweitzer

When God called me to be involved with MADD, I had no idea how rich my life would become. I experienced the incredible value of community as I joined with other volunteers whose lives had been impacted by a drunk driving crash in sharing our stories, processing pain, applauding healing and surrounding new victims with love and support. Starting while I lived in Maryland with my family, then, continuing with my subsequent move to Tennessee and eventually to Georgia, I sought ways I could serve in each local chapter. Consequently, I've made life-long friends. Sweet relationships were forged as we shared our stories at events, and connections were made that can never be broken. Chapter organizers and fellow speakers became like family to me. More than a fellowship of victims, we were victorious in what we had survived and cherished each other deeply.

During my work with MADD Tennessee, Millie Webb became a close friend and mentor. She had survived a horrific crash caused by a drunken driver. When her car burst into flames, Millie sustained burns over 75 percent of her body, as well as a broken neck. Her oldest daughter, Lori ,was only four years old at the time and died two weeks after the crash because of the burns that overwhelmed her little body. Millie also lost her 19 month-old nephew, Mitch Pewitt, who sustained burns over 90 percent of his little frame. Not only did Millie's husband Roy sustain burns to nearly half of his body, but she was pregnant with her second daughter, Kara who was delivered by emergency C-section at seven months of gestation. Millie's physical trauma was so great that it was a long while before she could even hold her newborn daughter. Kara is now legally blind, a condition attributed to damage caused during the crash. The courage and grace Millie exhibited in ministry to others reinforced my determination not only to survive, but thrive!

Beginning in 1991, Millie served on the MADD National Board of Directors and then became MADD National President from 2000-2002. She is still involved with the National Board and Tennessee Board of Directors. It was during Millie's tenure as national president that the President of the United States signed the .08 BAC Federal Law. This was a big deal because it lowered the level of blood alcohol content (BAC) considered to be driving under the influence (DUI) or driving while intoxicated (DWI). If a person is pulled over for erratic driving and their BAC is .08 or higher, they will be arrested. Prior to this new law, the BAC was .10. The new level is stricter and ensures more lives will be saved. My advice has always been not to drink and drive at all. There are many options available to avoid driving after drinking, so to get behind the wheel of a car when inebriated shouldn't even be a choice. The life of each driver is just as important as those he or she encounters on the road! My prayer is that folks will esteem their lives enough not to create a dangerous situation by attempting to drive after drinking. It took many, many hours of hard work to write this legislation and to lobby for the greater good. I was so proud of Millie and other shining stars of the MADD movement for representing victims of this violent crime and making our roads safer.

Another friend of mine, Brad Bulla, spoke alongside me on the Victim Impact Panels. He lost his 17-year-old son, Jedidiah, due to a drunk driving crash. The news that their vibrant teenager had died instantly when thrown from the truck he was riding in devastated Brad's family. I remember how Brad described falling to his knees in despair when he received the call about Jed. Losing his son in such a senseless way fueled a commitment to making a significant change in our culture. He began working with our local chapter of MADD and is currently serving on the National Board. He and his wife Tracy became very dear to me. Though these stories might be difficult to read, I want you to have a small inkling of the privilege it was to carry each others' burdens. Despite the pain of reliving our stories countless times, we were always thrilled when offenders told us how we impacted their lives. The looks in their eyes, and conviction in their words "to never drive drunk again" made our efforts more than worth it.

As I continued to perfect my speaking skills, I had several opportunities to share at churches and schools. My story often appeared in local newspapers and on tv news programs. One newspaper clipping dates back to 1995, when at 22 years old I first spoke on a Victim Impact Panel held in Trinity United Methodist Church in Salisbury, Maryland. Unfortunately, the reporter used the word "accident" in the title of the article, when in truth, a drunk driving impact is a crash and a crime.

A Picture of a Newspaper article from my first time speaking on a Victim Impact Panel. It was mistakenly titled "Accident." Drunk Driving is a crime. When sharing experiences, it is called a "Crash."

*Me with Vince Gill at a celebrity softball game to
benefit MADD near Nashville, TN.*

Ten years later, MADD Tennessee called me to interview on a local Nashville news station in preparation
for the upcoming Victims' Rights Week. It was in April,
2005, and we were enjoying gorgeous spring weather.
My heart was full of hope that our organization could
make even more of a difference by pushing awareness of,
and support for, victims of violent crimes. During that
interview I met another inspiring lady who also shared
her story. Verna Wyatt, petite in stature but mighty in
conviction, was the director of a local crime victim advocacy agency. Her family had suffered the tragic loss of
her sister-in-law, Martha, who was violently murdered.

Consequently, Verna truly understood the overwhelming needs of victims and their loved ones. Though we were serving in two different organizations, we made a strong connection. The interviews went very well and everyone was encouraged. Saying "good-bye" back then, I wondered if we would ever work together again.

Fast forward a couple years, and I received an unexpected phone call. It was 2007 when I picked up the receiver and heard Verna's voice on the other end of the line. She quickly reminded me of who she was and about the news interview we did together in Nashville. Then she began to explain a program their agency was doing and invited me to come speak. I was delighted to accept and quickly learned more about the victim impact class just starting in Tennessee prisons and jails. The emphasis of this class was not only that incarcerated men and women begin to understand the impact of their actions, but also would start to ask themselves how they came to be in prison in the first place.

Verna told me my story was so powerful because inmates saw not only the brokenness caused by a drunk driver, but also the power of forgiveness! She added that my listeners were privileged to see what a true survivor looks like: one who had been thrown into a pit of despair through no fault of her own, and despite much pain and suffering, prevailed to rise up again.

Not only did Verna encourage me, but so did her associate, Valerie Craig, Director of Education. They pointed out that through my passionate drive to overcome adversity, a beautiful strength was created in me that gives God glory because I boldly connect it to Jesus Christ. They cited the numerous grateful comments they received from prisoners each time I spoke. What a precious compliment. I was humbled and fortified to move into this next phase of my ministry.

Again, I needed God's strength and steadying calm as I stepped out of my comfort zone once again. The first time I spoke for Victims of Violent Crimes, the venue was much bigger than my previous visits to jails for MADD. The audience was made up of offenders who had committed all kinds of crimes. My prayer was that they could relate to how crime had totally changed my life. In preparation, Verna sent me a list of the strict rules regarding what I could and couldn't wear. This was prison protocol but also for visitors' safety as my first event was to speak in the men's prison in Tennessee. I was informed there would probably be 70 men in attendance and I should be "well covered up," no low-cut tops or short skirts. Fighting a sense of unease, I managed to control my butterflies with prayer, and met Verna and Valerie in the parking lot.

We walked in together, going through the security check point, and then through one locked door after another. Next to the main assembly room where I would be speaking, we waited in an adjacent area with a view of the prisoners taking their seats. That day we would address a Christian group called Men of Valor. Even so, when we were given the okay to walk forward, I battled apprehension as we passed by the men on the way to the podium. Yet the moment we started the program, the atmosphere of the room changed dramatically. I felt *life* and *good vibes* from the audience and noticed as I shared my story that the listeners were truly engaged.

After I finished, the response was amazing. I give God all the credit when inmates start responding with commitments to change their lives. A few of the men told me how much my story affected them and they wanted to know if they could sing a song for me.

"Of course!" I said.

They came to the front and began to sing. I don't remember the words or the title of the song, but their musical offering touched my heart deeply. Several in the audience told me they were really moved by what God had done in my life, the healing and forgiveness that shine through my testimony. What joy I felt in response to their comments. There's nothing more fulfilling than the assurance God had me in the right place to do His work, making a difference in the lives of others.

Despite the seriousness of addressing prisoners, we experienced some comical times too. On one particular day, when Verna, Valerie, and I entered the men's prison, a single line of inmates dressed in orange jumpsuits were walking down the long hallway. We could only guess where they were headed, maybe outside for recreation or for lunch. Half the men had walked past the point where we entered and were not aware of us. But all those at the back of the line turned their heads to take in the sight of three well-dressed ladies. Noting the inmates were distracted by us instead of watching where they were walking, the warden in charge quickly commanded, "Eyes forward! Eyes forward!"

I suppose the sight of us standing in the hallway was so unexpected that the men couldn't help staring. Just like in the movies, they promptly collided with the group of men who had stopped in front of them! We couldn't help but chuckle under our breath at the domino effect right before our eyes. As the men tripped forward, the warden barked once more, "Eyes Forward!" while he too suppressed a chuckle. We were grateful for any silly or cheerful moment to help lighten the somber mood of the prison environment.

I recently contacted Verna and found out she and Valerie are still working together. Their passion for victim impact facilitation led to the establishment of their own advocacy agency called Tennessee Voices For Victims. They continue to minister in prisons to incarcerated men and women, also focusing on restorative justice efforts with juvenile offenders and their victims. Their work is so needed in our society. When I think of the ripple effect of brokenness and sin, how wounded people make poor choices that devastate the lives of innocent strangers, I'm so thankful for the commitment of all my peers in the victim advocacy movements. If I still lived in Tennessee, I know I would be actively involved with them.

Indeed, the tireless efforts of volunteers who minister to inmates can really change the course of their lives for the better. The ultimate goal of victim advocacy groups is to stop repeat offenses, while offering inmates the opportunity to visualize doing something good with their lives when they get out of prison. My great joy, of course, was when I was encouraged to share how God worked miracles through my ordeal. I loved to share how He continued to touch my life: physically, emotionally and spiritually. Verna and Valerie never restricted me from sharing my faith, in fact they encouraged me to give glory where it was due, and to mention the forgiveness God worked between me and Steve. Truly, Jesus made it possible for me to walk and stand and minister. He is my everything!

There are so many more stories I could tell you. The numbers of people God has allowed me to speak to make it impossible for me to keep count. In recent years I've had the opportunity to serve with MADD Georgia, alongside Cynthia Hagain and Theresa DeWild. I've even shared my testimony several times with audiences at the Kings Bay Submarine Base near St. Marys, Georgia and Victim Impact Panels in Savannah, Georgia. Needless to say, throughout my journey I've felt God using me in ways I could never have imagined. As long as I keep my heart focused on Him, He directs me where He wants me to go.

For a long time I've sensed God wanting me to write this book so I can brag on His miraculous ways, reaching an even greater audience. Several folks along my path have encouraged me to do this, and I've waited on the Lord for His perfect timing. Then all of a sudden, I made another divine connection! Meeting Jessica Errico in Camden County, Georgia, was certainly Jesus' idea. She not only became a dear friend, but she caught the vision of what God has been doing in my life. Together we have labored to put my story in print, and there is still much we want to share with you.

So, buckle up, there are angels ahead!

Part Four

An Angel's Embrace

"For He shall give His angels charge over you, to keep you in all your ways."

Psalm 91:11

Have you ever encountered an angel? I don't mean the larger-than-life Hollywood version, dressed in shining robes and sporting large powerful wings, or the chubby cherubs playing harps on Valentine cards. No, I'm thinking of those real supernatural ministers of God who sometimes interact with us in human form. You might be surprised how many times they have crossed your path, transforming ordinary pavement into a miracle road!

God's ministering angels protect us and encourage us more often than we are aware. My testimony wouldn't be complete if I didn't stop for a moment and share more details of how angels have blessed my family.

The Bible is full of examples of angels interacting with us mortals. Over 300 times we read about how our great God has positioned them to bless us. There are a multitude of books available on the subject too. Still, some folks don't believe in angelic activity, so it's important to go to the Word of God for clarification about the reality of these supernatural beings. First and foremost, angels are created beings and never to be worshipped. On the contrary, their purpose is to worship God at His throne and to serve Him as messengers and ministers to His children. You may never see one with your physical eyes, but that doesn't mean they don't exist or are not working on your behalf. In fact, from Genesis to Revelation, God's Word proclaims His angels help us. As the Psalmist wrote in the verse above, "For He shall give His angels charge over you, to keep you in all your ways."

I don't know about you, but I find God's provision for us incredible! I already shared in chapter 2, how an angel appeared to my mom during my birth. In answer to Mom's prayer for help with her labor pain, a "nurse" came to rub her abdomen and comfort her. This young woman attended Mom throughout her labor, even accompanying her as far as the operating room for an emergency C-section. It seemed odd to Mom that this nurse never interacted with the other lady sharing her room. Then, when Mom tried to find her later to thank her for her help, no one knew of a nurse matching her description!

Nearly 15 years later, another angel ministered to us the night of the crash. This is what happened.

When the ambulance finally arrived at the hospital with my parents and Renea, they were each assigned separate rooms awaiting triage and X-rays. Renea, just barely 14 years old, shivered in the exam room, nervous and feeling so alone. Pain in her leg was excruciating, but as she heard my screams down the hall, fear about what was happening to me was almost overwhelming. Tears were rolling down her face when a nurse walked into the room. She had long wavy, sandy-blonde hair, was of average height, slender and beautiful. Though she was wearing a white nurse's uniform, she wasn't wearing a cap. She smiled sweetly as she approached Renea and my sister says she felt a peaceful, calming way about her.

"Is there anything I can do for you?" she asked.

"I just want to know how my sister is doing," came Renea's quivering reply.

The nurse reached out and began to rub my sister's leg right where it hurt. Everywhere she touched, the pain went away! Her words soothed even more as she said, "Your sister is going to be just fine. Watch and see!"

This nurse returned several more times to comfort Renea and speak encouraging words to her about my condition. Renea remembers it was every time fear and apprehension would start to grab hold of her, when no one else was in the room, that the nurse would come back. At one point, my sister noticed she wasn't wearing a name badge and asked, "By the way, what's your name?"

"Honey, you can call me anything you want to call me. You can call me Nurse Evans if you want," said the angel with a smile.

Nurse Evans never checked Renea's vital signs, nor gave her medicine, and was never present when medical staff were attending Renea. Her mission was to bring healing touch to my sister's leg and speak comforting words when Renea needed it most. Don't you know, when my folks and sister tried to find her a few days later to thank her for her help that night, no one in the emergency department recognized the name Nurse Evans. Renea's description of the nurse's physical appearance only brought puzzled expressions. That's when they concluded an angel had ministered to Renea, and her comforting words, "All will be fine. Just watch and see!" became even more precious.

Since the ministry of angels reflects God's constant care for us, I want to share a few more thoughts on the topic. John Calvin said, "Angels are dispensers and administrators of divine beneficence towards us. They regard our safety, undertake our defense, direct our ways and exercise constant solicitude that no evil befall us." Studying the nature of angels, I've learned they are worshippers of God Almighty, witnesses, messengers and mighty warriors. The Bible not only indicates that we have guardian angels, like the one that closed the lions' mouths when the prophet Daniel was thrown into the lions' den (Daniel 6:22), but they also do battle on our behalf. In 2 Kings 19:35, God sent an angel to deliver Israel from the Assyrian army. In one night 185,000 Assyrian soldiers were wiped out by angelic forces!

An account of the prophet Elisha is another fascinating story that refers to how angels are dispatched to protect us in time of need. Check out 2 Kings Chapter 6, where we read how the King of Syria purposed to attack Israel. Repeatedly, however, the prophet Elisha warned the King of Israel about the ambushing troops' location, ultimately avoiding attack. This angered the Syrian King greatly as he believed a spy was in his midst. When he was told the prophet Elisha was revealing their location through God's Word to the King of Israel, he ordered the prophet captured. Once the enemy army discovered where the prophet was, they surrounded the whole area.

It was night time and Elisha's servant was very afraid. Looking out at the city all he could see was the Syrian army encamped around them. Fearful for his life, the servant wondered aloud, "What are we going to do?"

"Do not fear, for those who are with us are more than those who are with them," reassured Elisha, as he prayed for the Lord to open the eyes of his servant to spiritual things.

2 Kings 6:15-17(NKJV).

The passage continues: "Then the Lord opened the eyes of the young man, and he saw. And behold, the mountain was full of horses and chariots of fire all around Elisha." God's angelic army surrounded Elisha, providing a buffer of protection from the enemy! The story continues with victory over the Syrians. How amazing! How encouraging to know God loves us so much that He has His angels keeping watch over us and fighting for us.

When we study the life of Jesus, we learn of the many times angels ministered to Him and others. Jesus is fully God and fully man, born of the Virgin Mary, conceived of the Holy Spirit. Before He was born, there was much angelic activity (Luke 1:26-38 NKJV). God sent the angel Gabriel to tell Mary what was about to happen. Gabriel told her she was blessed among women and added, "Do not be afraid, Mary, for you have found favor with God. And behold, you will conceive in your womb and bring forth a son, and you shall call His name Jesus. He will be great and will be called the Son of the Highest; and the Lord God will give Him the throne of His father David. And He will reign over the house of Jacob forever, and of His kingdom there will be no end." Though she was uncertain about how this was going to come about since she was a virgin, she wanted to bless God with her obedience and said, "Be it unto me according to your word." Then the angel departed.

An unplanned pregnancy in Jesus' time was quite a scandal, so God sent an angel to minister to Joseph, Mary's fiancé, as well. In a dream Joseph was told the child Mary was carrying was indeed the Son of God, and he should follow through in marrying her. Then we see angels delivering the message to shepherds the night Jesus was born. In Luke 2:8-15 (NKJV), the Bible says, "And behold, an angel of the Lord stood before them, and the glory of the Lord shone around them, and they were greatly afraid. Then the angel said to them, 'Do not be afraid, for behold, I bring you good tidings of great joy which will be to all people. For there is born to you this day in the city of David a Savior, who is Christ the Lord. And this will be the sign to you: You will find a Babe wrapped in swaddling cloths, lying in a manger.' And suddenly there was with the angel a multitude of the heavenly host praising God and saying: 'Glory to God in the highest, And on earth peace, goodwill toward men!'" In response to this glorious announcement, the shepherds hurried off to Bethlehem to greet their new-born Savior.

Throughout Christ's earthly ministry and even after His death and resurrection, angels played key roles of encouragement. They ministered to Him after His temptation in the wilderness (Matthew 4:1-11), they encouraged Him in the Garden of Gethsemane (Luke 22:41-43), witnessed His resurrection and announced it from His empty tomb (Mark 16:6-7), and ministered to His followers at His ascension (Acts 1:9-11). Additionally, God has commanded that angels worship Jesus as we read in Hebrews 1:6. They bow their knees to the King of Kings and Lord of Lords.

Another glorious truth the Bible affirms about the ministry of angels is they sometimes appear in human form to help us. Just as my mom and sister interacted with God's servants, Abraham and his nephew Lot did too! Read their stories in Genesis 18 and 19. God's angels came to Lot's rescue when destruction was imminent for Sodom and Gomorrah. They not only warned Lot to leave, protecting him from perverse and violent townspeople, but guided him and his family out of the city. Many centuries later, an angel was sent to rescue the apostle Peter from prison. In Acts 12:7 (NKJV), an angel came to Peter, struck him on the side lifting him up and said, "Arise quickly." Then the chains fell off his hands as the angel ushered him to freedom.

Furthermore, in the New Testament we are instructed to be prepared for heavenly visitors at all times. The Bible says, "Do not forget to entertain strangers, for by so doing some have unwittingly entertained angels" (Hebrews 13:2 NKJV). That passage speaks of angels being among us, embracing us with wisdom, encouragement and direction, even when we don't know their identity. My purpose in sharing these scriptures with you is to prove that angels are among us, seen and unseen. Though it is difficult to fathom and to keep at the forefront of our thinking, the spiritual unseen realm is as real, if not more so, as our physical world. God created angels as powerful spiritual beings, to watch over us and protect us in spiritual warfare. We should respect them for doing the work God sends them to do, always reserving our worship and praise for God Himself.

At the end of the Book of Revelation, chapter 22:8-9, right after Jesus says He is coming quickly, the angel sharing this incredible prophesy rebukes the apostle John for bowing low. Here's what the text says: "Now

I, John, saw and heard these things. And when I heard and saw, I fell down to worship before the feet of the angel who showed me these things. Then he said to me, "See that you do not do that. For I am your fellow servant, and of your brethren the prophets, and of those who keep the words of this book. Worship God."

Again, we are to worship God alone, but be grateful that He sends His ministering angels, our fellow servants, to bring us peace and comfort. Nothing is impossible for God! Not even the healing embrace of an angel named Nurse Evans.

Spiritual Boot Camp

"Jesus did not die just to make us safe. He died to make us dangerous."

Mark Batterson

In an increasingly politicized world, where people wield ideas and money to gain influence and power, it is easy to ignore the spiritual realm. However, God is spirit. He is the Creator and He desires mankind to seek Him, pursue Him and spend eternity with Him as His children. Consequently, an epic struggle is being waged for each human heart. Will we bow before our Heavenly Father, serve Him and enjoy Him forever? Or, will we resist His offer of peace and joy, pursuing our own agenda, intent only on gratifying what our carnal nature desires? The Bible depicts this grand conflict throughout its pages. The enemy of our souls is ever intent on causing us to doubt God. Is God truly who He says He is, is Jesus' atoning sacrifice enough and can we really trust God's promises?

These questions are at the root of mankind's yearning. Only a relationship with Jesus Christ can bring deep abiding peace and a blessed contentedness. This is known as assurance in Christianity. Assurance affirms God's love and His good intent for our individual lives, while confusion and doubt are pitfalls of which to be wary. The very fact that God sends supernatural angels to protect us, indicates our journeys include battles. The Bible explains that spiritual warfare takes place in the spiritual realm, generally unseen by human eyes, but influencing us just the same.

This may be news to some, but a true reality none-the-less. Satan was cast out of Heaven by God because of his prideful desire to be equal with the Almighty. Thus, he became the nemesis of all God's children. This arrogant angel is our foe, and though powerful, has limited abilities and authority; a fact he doesn't want us to believe. His strategy to keep us in bondage only works if we either: refuse to acknowledge he exists; or at the other extreme, fear he is too powerful to defeat. Though the battles against him and his demons are intense at times, with God's equipping, empowerment, and protection we are victorious! In fact, Jesus told his disciples in Luke 10:19 NKJV, "Behold, I give you the authority to trample on serpents and scorpions, and over all the power of the enemy, and nothing shall by any means hurt you."

The great news of the Gospel is that Jesus conquered death and nullified Satan's schemes once for all. In fact, the battles and skirmishes we encounter are opportunities for our Heavenly Father to train us and reveal His all-sufficiency. He is our Redeemer King and always victorious! No matter how hard or long a battle is, those who trust in Jesus as Savior have an inheritance that can never be stripped away and a home in Heaven with God as our ultimate reward. God has not left us uninformed about the challenges to come. He gives us instructions and examples from history to teach us and prepare us. That is why Bible reading is a must.

For instance, in the scriptures we are given a clear picture of how prayer moves God's Hand even when there is a delay. In the Book of Daniel, we learn how God's choice servant, the prophet Daniel, had been taken from Israel as a captive to Persia. In chapter 10, verses 2-13, Daniel had been in mourning over his people for three weeks, abstaining from choice food and drink, praying for God's guidance. On the last day of his fast, an angel appeared to him. In verses 12 and 13 (NKJV) we read this explanation of what occurred in the spiritual realm: the angel said, "Do not fear, Daniel, for from the first day that you set your heart to understand, and to humble yourself before your God, your words were heard; and I have come because of your words. But the prince of the kingdom of Persia withstood me twenty-one days; and behold, Michael, one of the chief princes, came to help me, for I had been left alone there with the kings of Persia."

The angel told Daniel that from day one when he prayed, God heard him and sent the return message with the angel. However, there was demonic interference as the principalities over Persia (the spiritual princes of the region) put up a fight. They fought against the angel in an effort to keep him from delivering the message to Daniel. Michael the archangel, a mighty warrior, showed up on the scene to secure victory, allowing the message to be delivered. This is a great description of what battles in the spiritual realm look like. Daniel did not give up on his fast, nor did he stop praying, even when he didn't hear an answer to his prayers. He kept praying, kept pushing forward, continuing to focus on God until his answer came.

We can certainly apply this to our lives today. It's often too easy to give up after the first day or so of prayer, thinking maybe our request isn't God's will, or that nothing will ever change. In general, we tend to be unaware of the spiritual warfare going on behind the scenes. The enemy wages war to keep us from our breakthrough. But take heart, we have spiritual weapons to win the battle. We are called to be overcomers! And by prayer, praise and putting on the armor of God we fight for what belongs to us.

During those long days in the hospital, I asked for prayer on a daily basis. My family prayed with me continually. I also loved to hear Mom read the Bible aloud. Almost every evening I asked her to read the scriptures to me and my spirit calmed as I sensed God's peace. Though I could certainly read God's Word for myself, it was soothing and powerful to hear it out loud. It relaxed me, eased my pain, and built up my faith as I focused on God's truth. And when we prayed together, I knew without a shadow of doubt, God heard my requests. I trusted He would move on my behalf and heal me. My family and I did not give up believing and asking. What we knew then, and have seen affirmed over the years, is that prayer and praise are powerful spiritual weapons. I love James 4:7 NKJV that says, "Submit to God, Resist the devil and he will flee." The enemy can't stand it when God's people pray, and praise God's Holy Name. Singing out the all-powerful name of Jesus is not only a battle cry, but a reminder that "He who is in you, is greater than he that is in the world" (1 John 4:4 NKJV).

A favorite Bible verse, one loved by many, is Psalm 22:3 NKJV which reads: "But You are holy, enthroned in the praises of Israel." The Living Bible puts it this way: "For you [God] are holy. The praises of our fathers surrounded your throne; they trusted you and you delivered them." How comforting to know that when we praise God, our words reach up to Heaven and He is present! He is our help in trouble, a strong fortress to protect us. In reading the words of His prophets, apostles and His Son, our hearts are fortified for the road ahead. He is mighty to save and deliver us because His promises are true.

What are your favorite Bible verses? Our victory depends on knowing God's Word, meditating on it and memorizing it. The apostle Paul wrote to the Ephesian church the following commands: "Stand firm...and pray in the Spirit on all occasions with all kinds of prayers and requests" (Ephesians 6:14,18 NIV).

In seeking God and trusting what Jesus did on our behalf, we have the assurance of the Psalmist who wrote: "I waited patiently for the LORD; He turned to me and heard my cry.

He lifted me out of the slimy pit, out of the mud and mire; He set my feet on a rock and gave me a firm place to stand. He put a new song in my mouth, a hymn of praise to our God. Many will see and fear the LORD and put their trust in him" (Psalm 40:1-4 NIV).

I lived this out and you can too! Calling on God's mighty Name and worshipping Him unleashed His blessing in my life. His healing touch restored my life and enabled me to serve Him by ministering to others. When I chose to focus on His goodness and proclaim His attributes, God gave me grace to cope with my long recovery. At times when my therapy was so painful and it seemed my ordeal would never end, He changed my perspective and helped me ward off self-pity. Prayer and Praise are the most powerful weapons in the universe because they invite (and depend on) the Creator's intervention, His mighty touch! Truly, He caused my feet to stand again and He put an even greater desire to praise Him in my heart.

The Bible says that, "the weapons of our warfare are not carnal but mighty in God for pulling down strongholds, casting down arguments and every high thing that exalts itself against the knowledge of God, bringing every thought into captivity to the obedience of Christ..." (2 Corinthians 10:4-5 NKJV). Those two verses contain volumes of theology, but simply put, spiritual battles can not be fought with conventional weapons or willpower. When we rely on God as our Deliverer, we will be astounded by how He fights for us and how He directs us.

I can't help but think about the power of praise evidenced by the walls of a mighty city falling down. Do you remember the story of Jericho and God's deliverance in the Old Testament? God had brought the Israelite slaves out of Egypt, through the wilderness, in route to the promised land. Yet, the peoples' grumbling and unbelief turned a journey of weeks into a 40 year odyssey. Still God stayed faithful to provide for their needs. Just prior to entering the promised land, however, their leader Moses died. Joshua was then given the mantle of responsibility to lead the Israelites across the Jordan River into their future. Fortified and instructed by the Angel of the LORD, Joshua issued divine directions on how they were to take the city of Jericho, their first obstacle in the land God promised them. The Almighty's orders sounded very weird indeed.

The army would not take the fortressed city by scaling its walls. Instead, they were to march around the impregnable compound once a day for six days to the sound of trumpets. Then on the seventh day, the army and priests carrying the Ark of the Covenant (who had accompanied them all week) would circle around Jericho six times in silence. On the seventh time around, they were commanded to shout loudly to the Lord at the sound of the trumpet. At that victorious shout, the strong walls tumbled down and the Israelite army overtook the city. The work of toppling those walls was done by faith, prayer and obedience. With a shout of praise to the Lord, victory was won!

The definition of praise is to honor, worship, and express admiration. When we pray for an answer to a problem, we should then begin praising God with expectation. Praise is a weapon always at our fingertips. When it's offered to God it makes the enemy flee. A New Testament example of this principle is found in the account of Paul and Silas recorded in Acts 16. They had been thrown into prison because they cast a demon out of a slave girl. The masters of this girl were furious because they had profited by using her as a fortune teller. With the demon gone she had lost this "ability," so they beat Paul and Silas with rods and had them incarcerated. But God had a plan!

Around midnight Paul and Silas began to pray aloud and sing praises to God. They took their eyes off their circumstances, off their wounds, their chains, and the dank prison walls, truly focusing on God. These servants of the Most High were fortified by singing hymns to our Heavenly Father, and their songs were a testimony to the other prisoners. As they sang, the earth began to shake so violently that the foundation of the prison trembled, doors opened and everyone's chains loosened! The other prisoners were witnesses to this mighty move of God and lives were changed! In reading the full account in Acts, we learn that the jailer in charge of the prisoners, along with his entire family, came to faith in Jesus Christ that very night. Talk about a mighty move of God!

Truly, our God is bigger than any problem we may encounter; and Jesus "is the same yesterday, today and forever" (Hebrews 13:8 NKJV). When we deal with circumstances by worshipping and praising God, they cease to have power over us. Pause right now and let that sink in. The Almighty God of the universe promises to shine through our troubles and deliver His people. What precious truth. Listen to the assurance evident in Psalm 91:14 where God is quoted saying, "Because he has set his love upon Me, therefore I will deliver him; I will set him on high, because he has known My name. He shall call upon Me, and I will answer him; I will be with him in trouble; I will deliver him and honor him."

God empowers us with His Word, through His son Jesus Christ, and by His Holy Spirit within us. Indeed, "The righteous cry out, and the LORD hears, and delivers them out of all their troubles" (Psalms 34:17 NKJV). As we determine to meet the trials in life with spiritual weapons, we become mighty warriors for Christ, able to defeat the enemy in the name of Jesus. And critical to our success is perseverance. Don't give up trusting and praising. Some battles involve a delay of God's answer, but just as Daniel persisted, we will prevail if we stand firm. Though at times you may grow weary in the battle, just ask a fellow believer to stand with you and help hold up your arms. God's army enlists the whole Body of Christ and we surely need each other.

Remember, God's provision is always perfect. Not only do we have His indwelling Holy Spirit, Christian brothers and sisters, the great testimony of godly servants like Daniel, Joshua, Paul and Moses, but we also have been given spiritual armor to wear. So, let's suit up, piece by piece...

Armor Up!

"All you have to do is show up, dressed up!"

The moment Steve's car crashed into us, we knew we were in a battle. Yet, we were not defenseless. The Bible says, "the battle is the Lord's" (1 Samuel 17:47 NKJV). In His perfect provision, God has given us spiritual armor to wear all the time so we can stand against the enemy's schemes. When we take the time to pray God's protective covering over us, we're reminded of His constant care. Then, focused on God, we are able to stand in the face of trouble and experience miracles.

The Apostle Paul's teaching to the church at Ephesus applies to our lives today: "Finally, my brethren, be strong in the Lord and in the power of His might. Put on the whole armor of God, that you may be able to stand against the wiles of the devil. For we do not wrestle against flesh and blood, but against principalities, against powers, against the rulers of the darkness of this age, against spiritual hosts of wickedness in the heavenly places" (Ephesians 6:10-12 NKJV).

Plainly put, in the challenges of this life, our battle is not against people. Though the actions of others cause all kinds of damage, it is the evil doer Satan working behind the scenes who is ultimately at fault. He also tempts us to give into our old sin nature which prompts selfish thoughts, words and actions. The key to successful warfare is knowing who our enemy is, and Paul delineates that we wrestle with spiritual principalities and the evil rulers of darkness in the spiritual realm. For this reason, he instructs us to dress in the whole armor of God and use the spiritual weapons at our disposal.

"Therefore, take up the whole armor of God, that you may be able to withstand in the evil day, and having done all, to stand. Stand therefore, having girded your waist with truth, having put on the breastplate of righteousness, and having shod your feet with the preparation of the gospel of peace; above all, taking the shield of faith with which you will be able to quench all the fiery darts of the wicked one. And take the helmet of salvation, and the sword of the Spirit, which is the word of God..."

Ephesians 6:10-17 (NKJV)

We are victorious when we suit up in God's armor, so, let's review each essential piece.

First, we apply the belt of truth. The scripture says to gird your waist with truth, or put on the belt of truth. Truth is essential for us to stand against the lies and deceptions of the devil. Truth keeps us from giving into the world's belief system. We are to navigate this life based on God's true Word alone, following Jesus' teachings and examples. Jesus says that He himself is truth. He proclaimed, *"I am the way, the truth, and the life. No one comes to the Father except through Me."*

John 14:6(NJKV)

Also, the apostle John wrote this about Jesus, *"And the Word became flesh and dwelt among us, and we beheld His glory, the glory as of the only begotten of the Father, full of grace and TRUTH."*

John 1:14(NKJV)

No wonder we need to put on Jesus (our way, truth and life) first! He has already won the war for us. By dying a sacrificial death to pay for our sin, and rising again, He provided His blood for our salvation and healing. This is the truth we hold on to, remembering that in the spiritual realm we are covered by the blood of Christ. It was Jesus who virtually held me together and gave me the ability to stand on His promises those long months of my recovery.

The second piece of armor is the breastplate of righteousness. The breastplate protects our vital organs, especially the heart. Putting on God's breastplate means guarding our hearts from Satan's attack. Righteousness is walking in right standing with God because we have been forgiven of our sins. It means doing what's right in His eyes, resisting sin and the pull of our old nature. Still, God's righteousness cannot be gained just by obeying the law, because at times we fall short of obeying His commands perfectly. Thank God, His righteousness comes through trusting in Jesus and not by trusting in our own works or in keeping the ceremonial law. It is received through faith in the person and gospel of Jesus Christ. In Paul's letter to the Philippians we read, "*...not having my own righteousness, which is from the law, but that which is through faith in Christ, the righteousness which is from God by faith.*"

Philippians 3:9 (NKJV)

Remember the account of Abraham, who became the father of God's chosen people? It was unwavering faith in the promises of God, being fully convinced that God's promises are true, that was credited to Abraham as righteousness. Paul references in Romans, chapter 4, God's promise to Abraham that he would be a father of nations. Abraham chose to believe God for the impossible. The scripture reads, "*And not being weak in faith, he did not consider his own body, already dead (since he was about a hundred years old), and the deadness of Sarah's womb. He did not waver at the promise of God through unbelief, but was strengthened in faith, giving glory to God, and being fully convinced that what He had promised He was also able to perform. And therefore 'it was accounted to him for righteousness.'"*

Romans 4:19-22 (NKJV)

Paul continues by saying Abraham's example is for us too. In their old age, Abraham and Sarah conceived a son just as God had promised. It is credited to us as righteousness when we also believe in the Son of God; when we trust that He died for us, is raised to eternal life and lives in heaven interceding for us! This is how you put on the breast plate of righteousness. Believe and receive that it is Christ living inside you by His Holy Spirit that makes you righteous. Believe and receive the promises of God as Abraham did. Since I chose to trust and follow Christ at an early age, I had the righteousness of Christ guarding me. It is Christ in me that stood strong, His righteousness kept my eyes trained on God.

The third piece of God's armor mobilizes our feet! The New King James version of the Bible tells us to "shod our feet with the preparation of the gospel of peace," which essentially means: put on God's peace and go preach the hope found in Christ. Don't be distracted by calluses or blisters, but be ready at all times to go and share the good news of Jesus. Our mission is to announce the Kingdom of God and share the truth of Christ. The Old Testament prophet Isaiah taught that the feet of those spreading the gospel are beautiful. *"How beautiful upon the mountains are the feet of him who brings good news, who proclaims peace, who brings glad tidings of good things, who proclaims salvation, who says to Zion, 'Your God reigns!'"*

Isaiah 52:7 (NKJV)

So, count it a joy to share the gospel of peace.

I think of the Samaritan Woman in John 4, and her unexpected encounter with Jesus. While she was drawing water from a community cistern under the scorching noonday sun, in an effort to avoid contact with the townsfolk, a conversation she had with God's Son changed her life forever. You see, Jesus was seated by the well waiting for her. When He revealed to her that He was the long-awaited Messiah, she excitedly put on her gospel shoes and ran to share the good news with all who would listen! Leaving her water pot behind, she ran proclaiming, *"'Come see a man who has told me all things that I have ever done. Could this be the Christ?' Then they went out of the city and came to him."*

John 4:29-41 (NKJV)

Because the woman was not afraid to testify about Jesus, many believed the truth about Him. The gospel of peace changes lives and saves souls! Just as the Samaritan woman was compelled to share about the Lord, I realized as I lay in a hospital bed that I too needed to share about God's goodness.

The next piece of our armor is the shield of faith. In Ephesians 6:15 NKJV we read, "Above all, take the shield of faith with which you will be able to quench all the fiery darts of the wicked one." Faith is essential when it comes to spiritual warfare. Faith is being sure of God's character and promises. When we stand firm, trusting in His promises, the devil cannot break through our shield of faith. The apostle John taught that our faith overcomes the world in 1 John 5:4 NKJV. He wrote, "For whatever is born of God overcomes the world. And this is the victory that has overcome the world—our faith." We are victorious when we stand strong in our faith that God is good and He rewards those who seek Him.

The scriptures affirm that without faith it is impossible to please God. In the Book of Hebrews, chapter eleven is known as the faith chapter. Several heroes who trusted God are listed there. We are reminded in verse 6, "But without faith it is impossible to please Him, for he who comes to God must believe that He is, and that He is a rewarder of those who diligently seek Him" Hebrews 11:6 (NKJV).

Faith is required in walking with the Lord. Through faith we overcome the challenges of life, it is a shield about us.

Though early Roman militia used their shields as offensive weapons as well as defensive ones, it's fascinating how they would overlap and sometimes lock their shields together to effectively protect their unit. When I apply this tactic to Christian life, I think of it as "linking our shields together." As Christians link their faith together in prayer, an impregnable wall is created against the enemy. Not only does faith form a powerful barrier but it is an unbeatable force as well. Jesus taught the following: *"Again I say to you that if two of you agree on earth concerning anything that they ask, it will be done for them by My Father in heaven."*

Matthew 18:19 (NKJV)

Praise God! Where any two agree, combining their faith, God will act. I know when I was in the hospital, it was our agreement and faith in Jesus that brought about so many miracles. It was in response to my faith and my family's faith, deliberately linking shields with other believers, that God brought victory. He took the awful thing that happened to me and brought about good for His glory. Hallelujah!

The fifth piece of our godly armor is the Helmet of Salvation. Jesus died for our sins and rose again on the third day. He did this to provide redemption and healing for all who will trust Him. We have to know that we know this truth. The helmet of salvation guards our minds spiritually, protecting the hope we have in Christ. In other words, after we receive salvation, we must renew our minds to be in line with God's Word. If your soul and spirit aren't filled with God's thoughts, the enemy can easily distract and discourage you with lies and deception. He will battle your mind, so your mind must be guarded by the truth of Jesus.

I love the way Romans 12:2 NKJV says it, "And do not be conformed to this world, but be transformed by the renewing of your mind, that you may prove what is, that good and acceptable and perfect will of God." If our minds are conformed to worldly ideas and desires, we cannot be victorious. We need an overhaul of our thoughts with the Word of God as our standard and basis for everything. God calls us to stand on His promises, believing they are true for us. The Helmet of Salvation is such a powerful piece of armor because when we dwell on God and His purposes, we are not vulnerable to the lies of the enemy. When you know that you know, the enemy cannot steal truth and wisdom from you!

From the age of four, when I saw Jesus hanging on the cross and He told me He loved me, my faith in what Jesus did for me was set in place. I am saved and I am whole. When the enemy came to fight against me and bring despair, I needed to refocus my mind on what Jesus did for me. When I put on the helmet of salvation, my heart and spirit were able to concentrate on my healing, getting well, getting out of the hospital, and fulfilling the purposes God had for me. I knew that I knew that Jesus was carrying me and that all would be well.

Last but not least, God has given us a very powerful weapon, the Sword of the Spirit. While the rest of our armor functions mostly as defensive protection, the sword of the spirit will bring the devil down and cause him to flee in terror. It is the Word of God. This is how the writer of Hebrews describes the Word of God, *"For the Word of God is living and powerful, and sharper than any two-edged sword, piercing even to the division of soul and spirit, and of joints and marrow, and is a discerner of the thoughts and intents of the heart."*

Hebrews 4:12 (NKJV)

Think about that for a minute. The Word of God is so powerful and sharp that it cuts both ways! As a discerner of thought, knowing the hearts of mankind, God's Word changes us even as it vanquishes the enemy. The Sword of the Spirit not only causes the devil to flee when we stand on and speak the Word of God, but it transforms us into mighty warriors for God's Kingdom.

It is our job to keep our swords sharp and learn how to wield them against the enemy. This requires daily study of the scriptures. To sharpen your sword, read the Bible every day, study, and ask God to reveal the truth of His Word to you. Don't seek just head knowledge or memory knowledge, but seek to really understand the Word. Ask God to open your eyes to His truth. *"Be diligent to present yourself approved to God, a worker who does not need to be ashamed, rightly dividing the word of truth."*

II Timothy 2:15 (NKJV)

This verse directs us to diligently study so we know what God says. Then we can stand on His promises and use truth to make the devil run away!

Jesus did this when he was tempted in the wilderness (Matthew 4). Every time the devil tried to tempt him, Jesus used God's Word as a weapon against him. He countered each suggestion of the enemy with the words, "It is Written..." After the third time, the devil left him alone. He couldn't continue to fight against a weapon that was cutting him to shreds. It is with the sword of the Spirit that we stand against the attacks and lies of the enemy. We are able to cut every lie down with the Word when we have studied it, know it and use it. The Bible was my go-to every day in the hospital. I needed Mom to read it to me. I wanted to hear it spoken. It gave me peace. I also knew it would make the devil flee. Fear and despair can't hang around when we apply the Word of God to our situation. I know because in the hospital I used God's truth against the lies of the enemy and miracles happened!

Now, this quick summary of the Armor of God is in no way a substitute for one's own study. Series of sermons and volumes of theology have been written to explain this phenomenal spiritual attire. Suffice it to say that as God's children we need to be clothed in His armor. It is vital to be held together by the truth which is Jesus. We put on the righteousness of Christ by faith and prepare to share the good news of the gospel of peace. We take our stand against the enemy's schemes guarded in faith, shields up! We train our minds to be in line with God's Word by focusing on scripture. Trusting that Jesus died for us and rose again, we commit to knowing God's Word, using it and speaking it. This is how God brought me through the crash and healed my body and emotions. My miracle road was possible, because when I armored up, He made me more than a conqueror.

There's a battle cry in the Book of Revelation that gives us assurance. I'm reminded that all who follow Christ can be assured of victory, for a voice from Heaven said this about the saints of God, "*...they overcame him [the devil] by the blood of the Lamb and the word of their testimony.*" Revelation 12:11 (NKJV)

Faith-Fueled Action

"Faith is not complacent, faith is action. You don't have faith and wait. You have faith and move."

-Betty Eadie

The word 'Faith' by definition is a noun. Grammatically speaking, a noun is a person, place or thing and functions very differently from a verb. To me, nouns are labels, names and titles, so I think the essence of the word 'Faith' breaks grammatical rules as we know them. As the quote above infers, faith includes movement... action. Though I'm not a wordsmith, I'm fascinated by how 'Faith' functions in a multitude of ways. I believe that spiritually, the word faith defies a strict definition.

For instance, faith is a trust or belief in something or someone. It describes allegiance, or dependence, or acceptance; such as I have faith in my mother's love or faith in my friend's goodwill. But spiritually, true faith includes action like a verb! The New International Version of the Bible tells us in Hebrews 11:1 that, "Now faith is confidence in what we hope for and assurance about what we do not see." Faith isn't static but dynamic. It is confidence based on trust, which is based on believing; an ongoing dependence on God's promises being true, and on His power to fulfill them.

There is a woman spoken about in the Book of Mark, who exemplifies the mystery of faith. We read her story in Mark 5:25-34 and learn how her faith required action. You see she had a medical condition for 12 years, one that was more than physically draining, one that made her a social outcast. She experienced bleeding that would not stop. On top of the suffering and weakness she endured for over a decade, such bleeding caused her to be considered perpetually "unclean." That meant she couldn't earn an income because it wasn't acceptable for her to be outside her home while suffering this disorder. Strict codes of hygiene as outlined in Leviticus chapter 15:19-31 kept her from interacting with the community. None of the many physicians she consulted could remedy her condition. The scripture tells us that she had spent all her money and was despondent of ever being cured. Not only that, but she was getting worse. I doubt we can really fathom the despair she must have felt. Her pain, bleeding, lack of social acceptance, and financial ruin would be enough to drag anyone under. Then, she heard that Jesus would be passing through town. His reputation had preceded Him.

On that momentous day, one that may have seemed normal to most, she said to herself, "If I can just touch the hem of his garment, I will be made whole (healed)." So, she did the unthinkable! She left her house in search of Jesus. Pressing through the crowd, risking scorn and ridicule, she reached out and touched the hem of his clothes. Instantly she was healed. Supernatural healing power flowed from Jesus to this woman, drying up the blood issue and healing her on the spot. The incapacitating problem she suffered for 12 years was gone in an instant when she followed up her faith with action.

When Jesus felt power leave him, he said, "Who touched me?"

His disciples replied, "You see the people crowding against you, and yet you can ask, 'Who touched me?'" So many people jostled them as they walked through the crowded street, surely it was impossible to identify any one touch. But Jesus knew.

She had only touched the hem of his garment, so what he felt was not a physical touch but a spiritual one. It was supernatural faith that caused Him to feel the power flow from Him to this woman. He asked who touched Him because He wanted her to identify herself. He wanted to bless her publicly, announcing to the townspeople that she was no longer unclean. When she confessed that it was her who had touched Him in search of healing, He said, "Daughter, your faith has made you well. Go in peace, and be healed of your affliction."

Notice that Jesus said to her, "Your faith." In this instance, He did not command her affliction to go by His faith or by praying for healing. She spoke in faith and took action. She received her miracle. Jesus honored her faith in His sovereignty. He blessed her with His peace and an assurance of continued wholeness.

From the minute of impact, that long-ago night in 1987, when metal collided with metal and my spine was severed in two, Jesus has honored my family's faith and prayers. We believed God for restoration and healing. And miracles happened! Faith requires action. It requires standing on the Word of God and not letting go of your request until you receive your miracle and blessing. Just like the woman healed of the issue of blood, I know from experience that God honors bold faith. Therefore, I stand on His Word and know God's promises will fully manifest in my life.

In Matthew 21:22 NKJV, Jesus said, "And whatever things you ask in prayer, believing, you will receive." And in Mark 11:24 NKJV, He also said, "Therefore I say to you, whatever things you ask when you pray, believe that you receive them, and you will have them." Both verses say pray and believe that you receive. That's action. Then you will have what you pray for! From the mouth of Jesus, God's Word says essentially, "Don't give up, keep believing and watch God work in your life!"

Remember Who it is you place your faith in. Our Creator God fashioned the world out of nothing. He spoke the universe into existence. He created something we can see with our own eyes out of something we cannot see. The visible created by the invisible. His voice, His command made it so. Therefore, faith is confidence in God's promises. Confidence in his Word. If He said it, then it is so.

When we stand on the assurance in His Word, saved by the blood Jesus shed for us, things begin to change and line up. A doctor's report may be considered a fact. A strained relationship may be considered a fact. Financial difficulty may be considered a fact. But when you apply God's Word over any report, over society, culture, the traditions of men, yes, over everything else in the world, then situations change. God's Word says that by Jesus' stripes we were healed, meaning we are healed.

When you stand on this truth, the doctor's reports begin to change and line up with the Word because we know God alone is our Healer. Finances line up as God is our Provider. Relationships change as we know God is our Father, our friend, our comforter, our everything. When you have confidence (faith) and hope in the Lord and his promises, then the truth of God's Word will change any situation.

This truth is evident in my life. On more than one occasion after the crash, God changed the doctor's report, leaving medical professionals astonished and unable to explain the miracles occurring in my body. My family and I stood on the promises of God, trusting Him to do what He said He will do. I became a walking miracle with bone supernaturally replaced in my back. There is nothing impossible for God when we trust him at his Word!

Faith is foundational to our walk with the Lord. It requires faith to be saved. You have to believe in the Lord Jesus Christ, who He is and what He did on the cross, in order to be saved (Acts 16:31). The great news is that faith is a gift from God. Paul wrote to the Ephesian church the following: *"For it is by grace you have been saved, through faith—and this is not from yourselves, it is the gift of God—."*

Ephesians 2:8 (NKJV)

And just like we are encouraged to ask for wisdom, God is pleased when we seek to increase our faith. Like the muscles in our bodies, which get stronger with use, faith is strengthened when we purposely exercise it.

Throughout my miracle road journey, I continually stepped out in faith. From speaking to my legs and seeing them move in the hospital bed, to circling around the altar with praying friends, my faith strengthened. Volunteering with MADD and sharing my story in many venues grew my faith as well. Then, in the late 1990s, after serving with MADD for four years, I received a great honor. I was nominated to be one of two representatives to speak on behalf of the Maryland Chapter of MADD at the Annual National Candlelight Vigil. This annual event changes location every year, drawing attendees from all the states in our country. That year, the Vigil was held in Detroit. I was allowed one companion, so I invited my sister Renea to accompany me to the event.

We flew into Detroit and stayed at the Renaissance Hotel across from the Convention Center downtown, all expenses paid. Taking the elevator up 23 floors, I marveled at the views of the city and the heights to which God had brought me. In the battle against drunk driving, I would represent all the injured victims in the state of Maryland that year. Another person represented the bereaved victims, those who experienced a death due to drunk driving. We were to address the convention with a brief testimony and light a symbolic candle on stage. There was just enough time before the event for a quick tour of the city, and then we needed to get ready.

Standing in line as the program began, I felt the familiar butterfly dance in my tummy.

I asked Renea to pray for me and was grateful for the prayers of my parents and friends back home. When it was my turn to take the stage, wrapped in prayer and God's goodness, my nerves calmed. God had called me to this task. He had a plan to use my story for the good of others and for His glory. I just needed to keep stepping forward on legs the doctors once said weren't supposed to work.

As each speaker came forward to share their story, a candle was lit for the state they represented. Just imagine how the "wall" of candles on the stage contrasted with the dim lighting in the assembly hall. There was a palpable reverence as the representatives of all 50 states addressed the audience, one by one. I felt the magnitude of what God had done for me, and in me, as a mantle of peace and hope settled softly on my shoulders. My sister lit the candle on behalf of all the injured victims of Maryland as I addressed the crowd of more than 500. My family had stood resolutely on God's promises, and now I had the privilege of standing up for so many lives affected by another's carelessness. Indeed, God was opening amazing doors for me to speak for Him!

Truly, faith equals believing and trusting, and requires action. We are told in James 2:17, that faith without action is dead. This means to receive what we pray for we have to act on our faith. We have to believe what God says is true and walk in the knowledge it will manifest in our lives. It is more than merely hoping something good can happen.

We are to renew our minds by studying God's Word, then take a stand on His promises and not back down. Don't let anything or anyone sway you from what the Bible says is true. Believe the Word, speak the Word, breathe the Word and live the Word of God. That's how we exercise our faith in our Almighty God. Miracles happen in response to faith fueled action!

Hope on Miracle Road

"Where Hope grows, Miracles Blossom."

Elna Rae

The roads we travel are as unique as our individual personalities and physical characteristics. As beautifully different as each snowflake design and every fingerprint pattern, the paths we follow through this earthly life are incredibly personal. The hills and valleys we traverse are watched over by our Awesome, Almighty Heavenly Father. He is always helping us and working ALL things for our good and His glory. This is the essence of what God was reminding Dad of the night of the crash...what Paul wrote in Romans 8:28 NKJV, "And we know that all things work together for good to those who love God, to those who are the called according to His purpose."

My miracle road began when I was born. Since my parents served God wholeheartedly, my life was always hemmed in prayer. I knew God was always for me, blessing me. Even the events on Highway 11, in Moselle, Mississippi on a warm autumn night, didn't take Him by surprise. When two cars crashed on that dark stretch of pavement, God was attuned to his people's hearts and prayers. As a result of His great mercy and love, before the cars even came to a halt, He already had an amazing plan in place; miracle after miracle, as I trusted Him. Praise His Name!

All of us have mountains to climb and battles to win. Be they physical, financial, relational or spiritual, the trials of life open our eyes to our need for God's help. They remind us that it is Christ in us who makes us overcomers. Author Sarah Young, in her bestselling devotional Jesus Calling, writes as if Christ is speaking to us directly: "When you became a Christian, I infused My very Life into you, empowering you to live on a supernatural plane by depending on Me." I have seen this truth play out during the course of my life, causing me to trust God's plans to always give me hope and a future.

The Old Testament prophet Jeremiah was called to serve God before he was born, and he loved God with all his heart. God used him to testify to an unbelieving society, to proclaim truth just as meaningful today as millennia ago! We read these words he penned and our hope is kindled:

"'For I know the plans I have for you,' declares the Lord, 'plans to prosper you and not to harm you, plans to give you hope and a future.'"

Jeremiah 29:11 (NIV)

Hope is an essential byproduct of faith. In Romans 5:5 NKJV we read: "Now hope does not disappoint, because the love of God has been poured out in our hearts by the Holy Spirit who was given to us." Whenever I felt lacking in hope, all I had to do was seek Jesus' face by reading the Bible. Since He has promised to never leave me nor forsake me, I only needed to remind myself of His truth. Then, setting my mind to serve Him and bring Him glory, I saw my hope multiplied. For instance, He gave me a wonderful opportunity to minister at an alternative school in Lawrenceburg, Tennessee.

MADD invited me to speak at a high school for students with behavioral issues. I don't remember who originally initiated the plan for me to address the youth there, but it was definitely a God thing. By then I was accustomed to hearing positive feedback from those who heard my story; this time however, I was addressing students after one of their classmates had died in a drunk driving crash. The teens were devastated. The mood somber. As I spoke, they were all on the edge of their seats.

When I wrapped up my talk, a teenaged boy approached me. He thanked me for coming and sharing what happened to me. Then he said, "You know, it's perfect timing that you came to talk to us today."

"Really?" I responded.

"Yeah, you see I had plans with friends to go camping this weekend. I know they're set on getting alcohol and drinking all weekend and probably driving too."

Without flinching, he looked me square in the eyes and said that in response to my story he made up his mind not to go. He decided right then and there not to participate in the drinking weekend event. He literally told me I probably saved his life.

What a precious moment to realize God had sent me there on this particular day, especially for this young man and generations that would follow from his life.

"Thank you for sharing that with me," I replied. "You've made the right decision to protect yourself and others. Please share my story with your friends to warn them how dangerous drinking can be."

He smiled, as he shook my hand, and said he would do it. Again, he thanked me for making such an impact on him and possibly saving his life. Truly it was the Lord who wanted to reach him that day! I was humbled by what God was doing. Hearing stories like his always encouraged me to continue sharing mine. That's really the purpose of this book: to reach as many folks as possible and make a difference in the lives of others.

Another mile marker on my miracle road, a further fulfillment of God's plans for me, occurred in the early 2000s. MADD requested that I speak for the National Lifesavers Conference at the Opryland Hotel in Nashville. The organizers of "the largest gathering of Highway safety professionals in the United States" wanted a victim to share his or her story with a panel of speakers. The conference attendees included highway safety officials from every branch (local, state and federal), as well as attorneys, victim advocates, law enforcement officers, and others. This annual conference serves to train first responders and support personnel from all over the country. I didn't realize then just what an honor it was to address this esteemed audience. Millie, my friend and mentor from my early years with MADD, told me recently that the invitation was a big deal.

I remember arriving at the hotel that beautiful sunny morning. Filled with hope, joy, and excitement, I made my way inside to the conference room where the meeting was to be held. Many rows of chairs were set up for the attendees. At the front I noticed a podium and a

ANGELA ADKINS

table for the panel speakers. Directed to sit at the table and await my turn to step up to the podium, I sensed the anticipation in the room. As the crowd filled the conference room, my stomach started flip-flopping and I reached for a glass of water on the table to wash down the nervous lump clogging my throat. Saying a quick prayer, I thanked God for this opportunity to impact those who serve our communities and asked for His blessing on my words.

Stepping up to the podium with my forearm crutches, I scanned the many, many faces of community leaders and officials. As I began to share my story, my nerves immediately calmed. I felt the tangible peace of God affirming this was what He wanted me to do. Though it was a multi-day conference for the attendees, I was only there for the one session. When it was finished, some of my friends from MADD who were there to support me gave me great feedback.

Leaving the hotel that day, I remember feeling a deep sense of satisfaction. I had fulfilled yet another task God set before me, for His glory. My desire was to always be available when MADD needed me to speak or volunteer. It amazes me that at the time I wasn't aware of how impactful some of these large events were. Only in writing this book have I come to understand the magnitude of the platform God had given me. He is so good. I trusted

Him to speak through me every time I had the occasion to share my story, and He did!

Sometimes we need a change of perspective to see the road God has marked out for us. For me, I needed to take to the sky to really appreciate all my Savior had been doing in my life. In August 1996, almost nine years after the crash, I was given the unbelievable opportunity to ride in the same helicopter that air-lifted me to the hospital. How humbling it was to see my life from God's vantage point. In response, my heart overflowed with hope and thanksgiving. This is how it happened.

My family and I were attending the annual General Assembly for our denomination held in Pennsylvania that year. While there, I was asked to share my testimony before the large crowd of pastors, Christian workers and their families. Bobby Tucker, a long-time family friend, came up to me afterwards and thanked me for sharing my story. At that point he was pastoring the same church in Mississippi that my dad had in the 1980s. Then he made the most surprising suggestion. Since he currently served as an EMT, flying the same helicopter that took me to the hospital that fateful night, would I like to ride in it again? My story had impacted him so much that he was willing to ask his superiors if a short flight could be arranged. This time it would be a Victory ride! Of course, I was game.

What a blessing from the Lord! My trip back to Petal, Mississippi, was a true homecoming. I was invited to speak at our old church, and then take a ride on Rescue 7. My sister Renea and a friend were with me for this Mississippi trip and they waited for me at the hospital helicopter landing pad. So different from my first flight, I was fully engaged and marveled at the whole experience. I've included some photos so you can see my smiling face.

Once onboard, I sat right behind Bobby as he flew us across town. Communicating via the headsets we both wore, he highlighted the difference in "take-off" for a helicopter versus a plane. He flew us at a low altitude so I could feel the speed, and then up into the sky at higher altitudes. Some moments felt like a roller coaster ride, followed by other moments we just hovered in place. So much like how we experience life at different times in our journeys.

With approval, Bobby not only took me into the air but also showed me the logs from October 14, 1987. I was able to read where they logged me in, as well as some notes written by the pilot and paramedic that night. It was surreal, to say the least, to experience all this from their perspective. He further explained about

the equipment in the chopper and some of the procedures they followed when they picked me up. As I looked
about the cabin, tears filled my eyes. I stared at the very
same stretcher they had strapped me to so many years
before. An image of myself laying there caused me to
turn my eyes away.

What a contrast! I couldn't help thinking about the
shape I was in back then in comparison to all the health
and mobility I've enjoyed since my recovery. I looked
out the window at God's beautiful creation, and felt en-
veloped by His peace. The whirl of the chopper blades
filled my senses, as I scanned miles of tiny houses, trees
and roads. I was overcome with the incredible reminder of how big God is, and how very small I am. Yet, He
cares so much for me. He not only spared my life and
performed miracles in me, but He opened wonderful
opportunities for me to serve Him!

Headphones on, prepping for a joy ride on Rescue 7.

*Rescue 7, I was standing by the gurney they had
me laying on when they airlifted me the night of
the crash.*

*The hope and faith I held on to back then, and I
still do to this day, comes straight from the words
of Jesus, "Anything is possible if a person believes."*
(Mark 9:23 NLT)

Now, many years later, I think of the poem "Foot-
prints in the Sand." If you haven't read this inspirational
poem attributed to several different authors I encourage you to do so. It illustrates for me how Jesus enabled
me to endure so many difficult challenges after the
crash. When I was in terrible pain and facing an uncer-

tain future, I don't believe Jesus merely walked beside me. No, I believe He lifted me up and carried me in His powerful arms. It was as if He looked deeply into my eyes and said, "It's alright, Angela. I've got you now. I know you are weak and worn, I'll carry you through."

True hope is found in Jesus alone. He came to give us hope and to give us abundant life (John 10:10). In fact, it is Christ living in us by His Holy Spirit that is the hope of glory (Colossians 1:27). When we place our hope in Him and in His Word, our faith increases and miracles manifest in our lives.

I was broken. There is no way I could have come back from all that happened to me in my own strength. Not even the great love of my family could bring me back from such a devastating ordeal. Only Jesus could make me whole again and He carried me through. Whenever you face a trial, or overwhelming challenge in your life, put your trust in Christ and stand firmly on His Word. That's where hope lies. He'll carry you through the deepest and darkest times of your life, placing you on your miracle road. Through steadfast faith and hope in Him, you will be victorious! Christ makes you more than a conqueror. I know, because he did it for me.

And so, it is my joy to echo the apostle Paul's benediction as I finish sharing this part of my story. I pray the following with my whole heart for each of you...

"Now may the God of hope
fill you with all joy and peace in believing,
that you may abound in hope
by the power of the Holy Spirit."

Romans 15:13 (NKJV)

Amen.

Epilogue

Dear Reader, thank you for traveling beside me on my miracle road. I thought our time together had come to a close, but then God brought to the forefront one more promise to share: the assurance of salvation. His promise of assurance is foundational as we journey life's road with Him! To trust Him completely is to rest in His sovereignty. Indeed, God knows the roads we will travel through life and He calls us to have faith in Him every step of the way... no matter what we encounter.

Assurance of God's goodness and in Heaven as our sure destination, keeps us on the path. The Hope of Glory guarantees us eternal life, and we can rest in the truth that "the best is yet to come."

Sixteen days after finishing this book, my mother Shirley Hicks stepped out of her earth suit and entered into the presence of God. This was totally unexpected. On a beautiful Sunday morning, just after getting ready for church, she collapsed. Mom finished her earthly journey and entered into her reward. Given how close my parents, sister and I have always been, the grief of losing her sweet, encouraging presence was more painful than I could ever have imagined. As my family clings to Jesus and the comfort He brings, Heaven is more real now than it has ever been before.

None of us know the date God sets for our earthly journeys to finish, so all of us need to be ready. God's ultimate plan for our lives is for us to join Him in eternity. He created us for fellowship and longs for us to love and worship Him. Yet, ever since the Garden of Eden, sin has been a barrier between us and our Heavenly Father. However, because of His great love for us, God put into place a costly, magnificent plan to redeem us. Through the death of His Son, Jesus Christ, we could receive atonement once and for all for our transgressions. By Jesus' selfless act of suffering and dying on the cross, He paid the punishment of death we deserved. In the Book of Acts (16:31NKJV) we read the following, "Believe on the Lord Jesus Christ, and you will be saved." The Gospel message is all about God's power to redeem us. Jesus was buried and rose on the third day according to the scriptures, displaying God's resurrection power! He invites us to trust in Him for salvation and in so doing join the family of God.

How can we do this?

To trust in Christ is: to believe what the Bible says is true, repent of sin (which means turn away from it), and ask Jesus to become the Lord of our lives. We read in Romans 10:8-9 NKJVthat if "you confess with your mouth the Lord Jesus and believe in your heart that God has raised Him from the dead, you will be saved. For with the heart one believes unto righteousness, and with the mouth confession is made unto salvation." Then a supernatural transformation occurs! He makes us new creations! Our spirits are quickened by His Holy Spirit and He guides us to live lives worthy of His Name.

As we walk out God's purpose for our lives, we share His love and light with the world. By our testimonies and life decisions, we are called to bring others to Jesus. Study the Word, connect with God in prayer, and watch the Holy Spirit do amazing things in you and through you. The greatest blessing comes when we leave this world and enter Heaven.

Believers are assured that to close our eyes in death means to open them in God's glorious presence! That's why it is so important to believe and receive Him into your heart now! In John 3:3 we read Jesus' assertion that unless a person is born again (saved) they will not see the Kingdom of God. I long to meet each of you who hold my book in your hands in Heaven one day. Assurance of your faith is essential to walking in the abundant life and divine health we see in the Word of God.

One of the hardest things to do in this life is bury a loved one. The grief and pain of missing them, comes in waves. But God. He knows the depth of sadness, the separation that death brings. Yet, He's always available to comfort us. Thomas Moore wrote, " Earth hath no sorrow that Heaven cannot heal."

When Mom was "promoted" to Heaven, my family knew with total assurance she is now with the Lord. Mom loved God and trusted completely in Christ. Her life among us confirmed her faith as she loved everyone who crossed her path. She never met a stranger and always found a way to share God's grace with others. Two of her favorite sentiments are: "Give it to the Lord" and "Jesus is coming soon. Be ready."

As I reminisce, tears fill my eyes. Mom was married to Dad for 50 years. Together they taught me spiritual truth and lived out authentic Christian faith before me. Mom always testified of her love for God and her family. She was eager to play the piano and sing for the Lord, ministering to others in His Name. And she anchored me during my long recovery, never leaving my side.

So, I have assurance that on September 2, 2018, my mom ran into the arms of Jesus! I know she is rejoicing in His presence and enjoying the company of loved ones who went on ahead of her. I have the same assurance about my destination. One day, when my journey is complete, I will join my Savior in Heaven and be reunited with Mom and others! So, I hold fast to this Hope of Glory, knowing that Christ lives in me now and will bring me home to be with Him someday. Will you be there too?

You may have attended church all your life but never asked Jesus to be your Savior. If so, you can do it right now. A simple prayer from a humble heart is the key to receiving Jesus. If you're ready, use the following prayer as a model; but don't just read it, pray it from your heart. When you mean what you say when you pray, you will be forgiven of your sins and Christ will enter your life. He will lovingly change your perspective and priorities and give you hope. Pray something like this:

"Father, I am sorry for my sins. I ask you to forgive me of all my sins. I believe that Jesus died for me, that he was beaten and nailed to a cross for my sins. I believe that Jesus rose from the dead on the third day and is sitting at Your right hand, interceding for me right now. I ask Him to come into my heart, live inside me, and make me new.

Thank you God for hearing and answering my prayer in Jesus Name!

I love you and I praise you in Jesus Name! Amen!"

If you prayed this prayer or something similar, really meaning it from your heart, you can be assured that Jesus by His Holy Spirit now lives in your heart! Welcome to the Kingdom of God! Your miracle road has just begun and will unfold as you pray! Study the Bible and find a good church where God's Word is taught. Best of all, you can be assured of a place with God in Heaven. Someday I'll meet you there! Praise God!

Scriptures for Healing

Read these scriptures, meditate on them and memorize them. Pray through these verses and speak them over your life because *"faith comes by hearing, and hearing by the word of God"* (Romans 10:17 NKJV). When you get it in your heart and mind that this is the Word of God for you, He will work through His Word and your life will change. Your circumstance will change for your good and to the glory of God. As you meditate on these scriptures, trust the work has already been done by the sacrifice Jesus made for you. He paid the price for your healing! By Jesus' stripes you ARE healed! I'm in agreement with you for your healing to manifest in your body in Jesus Name! It is done! Stand firm on Christ's faithfulness and walk in victory!

Blessings,
Angela Adkins

"….Do not be afraid. Stand firm and you will see the deliverance the Lord will bring you today. The Egyptians [*sickness, disease, oppression, bondage*] you see today you will never see again. The Lord will fight for you; you need only to be still."

Exodus 14:13-14 NIV

"…For I am the LORD who heals you."

Exodus 15:26 NKJV

"So you shall serve the LORD your God, and He will bless your bread and your water. And I will take sickness away from the midst of you."

Exodus 23:25 NKJV

"And the LORD will take away from you all sickness, and will afflict you with none of the terrible diseases of Egypt which you have known…."

Deuteronomy 7:15 NKJV

"Delight yourself also in the LORD, And He shall give you the desires of your heart."

Psalms 37:4 NKJV

"The Lord sustains them on their sickbed and restores them from their bed of illness."

Psalm 41:3 NIV

"Because you have made the LORD, who is my refuge, Even the Most High, your dwelling place, No evil shall befall you, Nor shall any plague come near your dwelling;"

Psalms 91:9-10 NKJV

"With long life I will satisfy him, And show him [*referring to children of God, male and female, him and her*] My salvation."

Psalms 91:16 NKJV

"Bless the LORD, O my soul, And forget not all His benefits: Who forgives all your iniquities, Who heals all your diseases, Who redeems your life from destruction, Who crowns you with lovingkindness and tender mercies, Who satisfies your mouth with good things, So that your youth is renewed like the eagle's."

Psalms 103:2-5 NKJV

"Then they cried out to the LORD in their trouble, And He saved them out of their distresses. He sent His word and healed them, And delivered them from their destructions."

Psalms 107:19-20 NKJV

"Trust in the LORD with all your heart, And lean not on your own understanding; In all your ways acknowledge Him, And He shall direct your paths. Do not be wise in your own eyes; Fear the LORD and depart from evil. It will be health to your flesh, And strength to your bones."

Proverbs 3:5-8 NKJV

"My son, give attention to my words; Incline your ear to my sayings. Do not let them depart from your eyes; Keep them in the midst of your heart; For they are life to those who find them, And health to all their flesh."

Proverbs 4:20-22 NKJV

"Surely He has borne our griefs And carried our sorrows; Yet we esteemed Him stricken, Smitten by God, and afflicted. But He was wounded for our transgressions, He was bruised for our iniquities; The chastisement for our peace was upon Him, And by His stripes we are healed."

Isaiah 53:4-5 NKJV

"No weapon [the enemy uses sickness as a weapon] formed against you shall prosper....This is the heritage of the servants of the LORD..."

Isaiah 54:17 NKJV

"So shall My word be that goes forth from My mouth; It shall not return to Me void, But it shall accomplish what I please, And it shall prosper in the thing for which I sent it." [*Speak the Word and promises of God. It will set out and accomplish what God says in His Word.*]

Isaiah 55:11 NKJV

"Then your light shall break forth like the morning, Your healing shall spring forth speedily, And your righteousness shall go before you; The glory of the LORD shall be your rear guard."

Isaiah 58:8

"For I know the thoughts that I think toward you, says the LORD, thoughts of peace and not of evil, to give you a future and a hope." [*God has great plans for us, to prosper us and not harm us, to give us a hope and a future.*]

Jeremiah 29:11 NKJV

"For I will restore health to you And heal you of your wounds,' says the LORD..."

Jeremiah 30:17 NKJV

"For I am the LORD, I do not change; Therefore you are not consumed..."

Malachi 3:6 NKJV

"Your kingdom come. Your will be done ON earth AS IT IS IN Heaven." [*No sickness or disease exist in Heaven, so he tells us to pray for His Kingdom on earth as it is in Heaven. Amen!*]

Matthew 6:10 NKJV

"Ask, and it will be given to you; seek, and you will find; knock, and it will be opened to you. For everyone who asks receives, and he who seeks finds, and to him who knocks it will be opened. Or what man is there among you who, if his son asks for bread, will give him a stone? Or if he asks for a fish, will he give him a serpent? If you then, being evil, know how to give good gifts to your children, how much more will your Father who is in heaven give good things to those who ask Him!"

Matthew 7:7-11 NKJV

"When evening had come, they brought to Him many who were demon-possessed. And He cast out the spirits with a word, and healed all who were sick, that it might be fulfilled which was spoken by Isaiah the prophet, saying: "He Himself took our infirmities And bore our sicknesses."

Matthew 8:16-17 NKJV

"Then Jesus went about all the cities and villages, teaching in their synagogues, preaching the gospel of the kingdom, and healing every sickness and every disease among the people."

Matthew 9:35 NKJV

"Then great multitudes came to Him, having with them the lame, blind, mute, maimed, and many others; and they laid them down at Jesus' feet, and He healed them. So the multitude marveled when they saw the mute speaking, the maimed made whole, the lame walking, and the blind seeing; and they glorified the God of Israel."

Matthew 15:30-31 NKJV

"And I will give you the keys of the kingdom of heaven, and whatever you bind on earth will be bound in heaven, and whatever you loose on earth will be loosed in heaven." [*This is big. Jesus gave the keys to the kingdom of Heaven to His church and believers. He placed authority to bind-(not allow) or loose-(allow) things in our lives. We have authority in Jesus Name to not allow anything from the enemy such as sickness and disease in our lives. Use the God given authority in Jesus Name to speak healing and restoration.*]

Matthew 16:19 NKJV

"So Jesus said to them, "Because of your unbelief; for assuredly, I say to you, if you have faith as a mustard seed, you will say to this mountain, 'Move from here to there,' and it will move; and nothing will be impossible for you."

Matthew 17:20 NKJV

"Assuredly, I say to you, whatever you bind on earth will be bound in heaven, and whatever you loose on earth will be loosed in heaven." [*He gives us the authority and freedom to allow or not allow things in our life. We either bind or loose.*]

Matthew 18:18 NKJV

"Again I say to you that if two of you agree on earth concerning anything that they ask, it will be done for them by My Father in heaven."

Matthew 18:19 NKJV

"But Jesus looked at them and said to them, "With men this is impossible, but with God all things are possible."

Matthew 19:26 NKJV

"So Jesus answered and said to them, "Assuredly, I say to you, if you have faith and do not doubt, you will not only do what was done to the fig tree, but also if you say to this mountain, 'Be removed and be cast into the sea,' it will be done. And whatever things you ask in prayer, believing, you will receive."

Matthew 21:21-22 NKJV

"And He said to her, "Daughter, your faith has made you well. Go in peace, and be healed of your affliction."

Mark 5:34 NKJV

"Jesus said to him, "If you can believe, all things are possible to him who believes."

Mark 9:23 NKJV

"So Jesus answered and said to them, "Have faith in God. For assuredly, I say to you, whoever says to this mountain [a mountain in your life could be sickness, disease, oppression, anything blocking your blessings], 'Be removed and be cast into the sea,' and does not doubt in his heart, but believes that those things he says will be done, he will have whatever he says. Therefore, I say to you, whatever things you ask when you pray, believe that you receive them, and you will have them."

Mark 11:22-24 NKJV

"And these signs will follow those who believe: In My name they will cast out demons; they will speak with new tongues; they will take up serpents; and if they drink anything deadly, it will by no means hurt them; they will lay hands on the sick, and they will recover."

Mark 16:17-18 NKJV

"For with God nothing will be impossible."

Luke 1:37 NKJV

"Whatever city you enter, and they receive you, eat such things as are set before you. And heal the sick there, and say to them, 'The kingdom of God has come near to you.'"

Luke 10:8-9 NKJV

"Behold, I give you the authority to trample on serpents and scorpions, and over ALL the power of the enemy, and nothing shall by any means hurt you."

Luke 10:19 NKJV

"But when Jesus saw her, He called her to Him and said to her, "Woman, you are loosed from your infirmity." And He laid His hands on her, and immediately she was made straight, and glorified God."

Luke 13:12-13 NKJV

"The thief does not come except to steal, and to kill, and to destroy. I have come that they may have life, and that they may have it more abundantly."

John 10:10 NKJV

"Most assuredly, I say to you, he who believes in Me, the works that I do he will do also; and greater works than these he will do, because I go to My Father. And whatever you ask in My name, that I will do, that the Father may be glorified in the Son. If you ask anything in My name, I WILL do it."

John 14:12-14 NKJV

"If you abide in Me, and My words abide in you, you will ask what you desire, and it shall be done for you."

John 15:7 NKJV

"And in that day you will ask Me nothing. Most assuredly, I say to you, whatever you ask the Father in My name He will give you. Until now you have asked nothing in My name. Ask, and you will receive, that your joy may be full."

John 16:23-24 NKJV

"Now, Lord, look on their threats, and grant to Your servants that with all boldness they may speak Your word, by stretching out Your hand to heal, and that signs and wonders may be done through the name of Your holy Servant Jesus."

Acts 4:29-30 NKJV

"How God anointed Jesus of Nazareth with the Holy Spirit and with power, who went about doing good and healing all who were oppressed by the devil, for God was with Him."

Acts 10:38 NKJV

"He is our father in the sight of God, in whom he believed—the God who gives life to the dead and calls into being things that were not."

Romans 4:17 NIV

"Yet he did not waver through unbelief regarding the promise of God, but was strengthened in his faith and gave glory to God, being fully persuaded that God had power to do what he had promised."

Romans 4:20-21 NIV

"Christ has redeemed us from the curse of the law, having become a curse for us (for it is written, "Cursed is everyone who hangs on a tree"),"

Galatians 3:13 NKJV

"Now to Him who is able to do exceedingly abundantly above all that we ask or think, according to the power that works in us,"

Ephesians 3:20 NKJV

"Being confident of this very thing, that He who has begun a good work in you will complete it until the day of Jesus Christ;"

Philippians 1:6 NKJV

"But without faith it is impossible to please Him, for he who comes to God must believe that He is, and that He is a rewarder of those who diligently seek Him."

Hebrews 11:6 NKJV

"Jesus Christ is the same yesterday, today, and forever." [*Jesus hasn't changed. He is still in the healing business.*]

Hebrews 13:8 NKJV

"Is anyone among you sick? Let him call for the elders of the church, and let them pray over him, anointing him with oil in the name of the Lord. And the prayer of faith will save the sick, and the Lord will raise him up. And if he has committed sins, he will be forgiven. Confess your trespasses to one another, and pray for one another, that you may be healed. The effective, fervent prayer of a righteous man avails much."

James 5:14-16 NKJV

"Who Himself bore our sins in His own body on the tree, that we, having died to sins, might live for righteousness— by whose stripes you were healed." [*You were healed means you are healed. Jesus already paid the price for healing, so it is done.*]

I Peter 2:24 NKJV

"Now this is the confidence that we have in Him, that if we ask anything according to His will, He hears us. [*His will, according to the Word and life of Jesus, is healing and divine health. To walk in fullness of life for His service.*] And if we know that He hears us, whatever we ask, we know that we have the petitions that we have asked of Him."

I John 5:14-15 NKJV

"Beloved, I pray that you may prosper in all things and be in health, just as your soul prospers."

III John 1:2 NKJV

About the Authors

Angela Adkins is a speaker, writer, Certified Biblical Health Coach, mentor, and leader. She is also a victim/survivor of a DUI crash. She shares her story to impact society by warning folks not to drink and drive; as well as bragging on our supernatural God. Her message revolves around the dangers of drunk driving and the incredible faithfulness of God to heal and restore. Additionally, Angela emphasizes the healing power of forgiveness. She forgave the drunk driver who nearly killed her due to his poor choices. Her great hope is for many readers to join her on her Miracle Road.

A volunteer and victim advocate for Mothers Against Drunk Driving, Angela has served as a spokesperson for MADD in Maryland, Tennessee, and Georgia. She received the great honor to represent them at two national conventions: the Life Saver's Conference in Nashville, Tennessee, and the National Candlelight Vigil in Detroit, Michigan. As well as speaking for MADD, she has shared her story in churches, schools and prisons. Over the years, Angela has blogged about her healing and faith on social media, and has appeared on television and radio interviews. She has two Public Service Announcements to her credit: one for MADD Lower Eastern Shore of Maryland and the other for the Highway Safety Program.

If you would like to contact Angela, she can be reached through her social media sites at *https://www.facebook.com//AngelasMiracleRoad* as well as *https://instagram.com/angela_adkins_*.

Jessica Errico is an author and speaker as well. She is a former pregnancy care center director with several articles and four books to her credit, most notably *THE MOTHER GAP: A Daughter's Search for Connection*. Jessica enjoys writing memoirs, especially those that deal with faith and forgiveness. She is a graduate of Dickinson College in Carlisle, Pennsylvania, and was inducted as a member of American Pen Women. Her personal journey of faith led her to do missionary work in Mazatlán, México, as well as full-time pastoral ministry alongside her husband in Austin, Texas and Deltona, Florida.

Jessica currently writes the Religion Column for the Tribune & Georgian weekly newspaper in Southeastern Coastal, Georgia. As a long-time Bible student, she leads a discussion group for Bible Study Fellowship and serves in her local church.

If you would like to contact Jessica, you can email her at *Jessica.errico78@gmail.com* or reach her on her Facebook Page, *The Mother Gap.*

CPSIA information can be obtained
at www.ICGtesting.com
Printed in the USA
BVHW041814151219
566754BV00014B/501/P